PRAISE FOR

MEET THE DEPLORABLES

"A rollicking ride through Trumpland; Leon takes you on a tour of the stranger side of the States. By turns laugh-out-loud funny and poignant, it's a vital guide to understanding what is happening in America today."
–**Harriet Alexander**
US Correspondent for *The Daily Telegraph*

"If you've had the courage to peek out of your asshole and take a gander at our devolving America, you won't be shocked the evils and inequities that Harmon Leon takes to task in this book. But you'll be amazed how Leon's hilarious subterfuge of a collapsed system can make us laugh as we slowly swirl down the muddy toilet."
–**Doug Stanhope**
author of *This Is Not Fame: A "From What I Re-Memoir"*

"Anyone can mock their ideological enemies, but Harmon Leon does something revolutionary here—he actually gets to know them. A natural, endlessly engaging storyteller, Leon's forays into Trump America are fascinating, funny, and incisive. Gonzo journalism at its finest."
–**Davy Rothbart**
creator of *Found Magazine*, author of *My Heart Is an Idiot*

"I got more of a sense of Trump's voters from [*Meet the Deplorables*] than from a lot of other reporting."
–**Nancy Updike**
producer of *This American Life*

ALSO BY HARMON LEON

Tribespotting:
Undercover Cult(ure) Stories

The American Dream:
Walking in the Shoes of Carnies, Arms Dealers, Immigrant Dreamers,
Pot Farmers, and Christian Believers

The Infiltrator:
My Undercover Exploits in Right-Wing America

Republican Like Me
:Infiltrating Red-State, White-Ass, and Blue-Suit America

The Harmon Chronicles

National Lampoon's Road Trip USA

The Brothers Rjukerooka

ALSO BY TED RALL

Revenge of the Latchkey Kids

To Afghanistan and Back

The Year of Loving Dangerously

After We Kill You, We Will Welcome You Back as Honored Guests: Unembedded in Afghanistan

The Anti-American Manifesto

The Book of Obama: How We Went From Hope and Change to the Age of Revolt

Snowden

Bernie

Trump

Francis, the People's Pope

MEET THE DEPLORABLES
INFILTRATING TRUMP AMERICA

MEET THE DEPLORABLES
INFILTRATING TRUMP AMERICA

BY HARMON LEON
AND TED RALL

39 WEST PRESS

39 WEST PRESS
Kansas City, MO
www.39WestPress.com

39 WEST
PRESS

Copyright © 2019 by Harmon Leon & Ted Rall

Harmon Leon Website: www.harmonleon.com
Ted Rall Online: www.rall.com

All rights reserved.

No part of this book may be reproduced, scanned, or distributed in any printed or electronic form, including information storage and retrieval systems, without permission. Please do not participate in or encourage piracy of copyrighted materials in violation of the authors' rights.

Please purchase only authorized editions.

First Edition: July 2019

ISBN: 978-1-946358-22-6

Library of Congress Control Number: 2017960409

10 9 8 7 6 5 4 3 2 1

Book Design: j.d.tulloch
Front Cover Design/Back Cover Cartoon: Ted Rall
Edits: Helen A.S. Popkin, Ted Rall, j.d.tulloch

39WP-23-P-BW

To the people of the future:

sorry.

CONTENTS

FOREWORD: THE TRUTH IS SCARY ... xv
PREFACE: WHERE OTHERS NOT DARE ... xx

Part One: Pure Crazy Trump Fanatics
INTRODUCTION: AMERICANS ARE STUPID. SO WHAT? ... 3
CHAPTER 1: TRUMP: THE ROCK & ROLL MUSE ... 7
CHAPTER 2: INK ME SOME TRUMP ... 15
CHAPTER 3: KNOCKING ON DOORS FOR TRUMP ... 26

Part Two: Build a Wall and Get 'Em Out
INTRODUCTION: TRUMP ISN'T BLUFFING ... 37
CHAPTER 4: ISLAMOPHOBES LOVE COOKIES ... 41
CHAPTER 5: ANGRY VILLAGERS CHASING ALIENS ... 50
CHAPTER 6: KKK RESTAURANTS MAKE GREAT PIES ... 61
CHAPTER 7: MUSLIM? NO GUNS FOR YOU! ... 67

Part Three: A Match Made in Heaven
INTRODUCTION: DON'T WORRY, TRUMP IS TOAST ... 75
CHAPTER 8: BEST LITTLE HELL HOUSE IN TEXAS ... 79
CHAPTER 9: HE BLINDED ME WITH BIBLICAL SCIENCE ... 87
CHAPTER 10: IT'S A PURITY RING THANG ... 96
CHAPTER 11: UNBORN JESUS & THE GRIM REAPER ... 104
CHAPTER 12: HIT ME WITH YOUR BEST EX-GAY SHOT ... 114

Part Four: Don't Take Away Our Guns
INTRODUCTION: ARMED TO THE TEETH ... 127
CHAPTER 13: NOT ON OUR WATCH ... 131
CHAPTER 14: JANIE GOT A GUN ... ON FACEBOOK ... 141
CHAPTER 15: IT'S A SHOTGUN WEDDING, LITERALLY ... 150

Part Five: Making America Great Again

INTRODUCTION: THE TSUNAMI IS COMING	161
CHAPTER 16: HERE COMES THE REPO MAN	167
CHAPTER 17: FEAR & LOATHING BENEATH LAS VEGAS	177
CHAPTER 18: THE SMELL OF METH IN THE MORNING	186
CHAPTER 19: KNIGHTS IN SHINING WHITE JUMPSUITS	196
CHAPTER 20: SHOUT AT THE DEVIL	202
AFTERWORD: THANKS TO TRUMP, A NEW LEFT RISES	209
ACKNOWLEDGMENTS	213
IMAGE CREDITS	215
ABOUT THE AUTHORS	217

EDITORS NOTE:
**PARTS ONE–FIVE INTRODUCTIONS BY TED RALL
CHAPTERS 1–20 BY HARMON LEON**

You know, to just be grossly generalistic, you could put half of Trump's supporters into what I call the basket of deplorables. Right? The racist, sexist, homophobic, xenophobic, Islamaphobic—you name it. And unfortunately there are people like that. And he has lifted them up.

–Hillary Rodham Clinton

FOREWORD

THE TRUTH IS SCARY

HARMON LEON (PICTURED ABOVE) is a national treasure—
and not like the Nicholas Cage movie, like for real. I knew
it the first time I read one of his infiltration pieces in *Might*,
which was a magazine you might have read or at least heard about—
especially if you were a Gen X white male and lived in or around San
Francisco in the mid-1990s.

During that time, the United States was coming out of a long
recession. Dot-Com Boom 1.0 was revving up, but the economy still
sucked. For the *Might* story, Harmon got himself a job at a Jack in the
Box in San Francisco with the self-appointed mission: see how fast he
could get himself fired from this shitty job.

Harmon acted like a colossal asshole but couldn't get himself fired.
Eventually, he gave up and left mid-shift.

Now that I've known Harmon for many years, I think that I finally
understand why his boss didn't let him go: he's an incredibly chill guy,
so likable that people just enjoy having him around.

I am not like that at all. Therefore, I am in awe of how his low-key energy allows him to blend in with people who, under different circumstances—i.e., if I tried to pull the same kind of shit—might beat him up.

Don't get me wrong: I, too, can mix with a surprising array of people. I've talked to members of the Taliban about what makes a girl hot—and lived to write about it. But Harmon has a *gift*. He can go anywhere, be with anyone, say anything—and everyone, anyone, wherever, whenever will be totally okay with him. If someday this infiltration shtick ever fizzles out, Harmon easily could get a job as an undercover agent.

There are other infiltrators. But none possess Harmon's sense of humor or his talent at getting just about anyone to open up. He is uniquely qualified to explore cultures and subcultures that others find incomprehensible or impenetrable.

A decade before I met Harmon, I was a loan officer at a Japanese bank's New York branch and had my first personal interaction with Donald J. Trump. My boss informed me that the Trump Organization was looking for backing—the sum requested, as I recall, was twenty-five million dollars—for a casino project called the Taj Mahal in Atlantic City, New Jersey.

My boss asked me to crunch the numbers—to see whether the Taj Mahal was financially viable and thus whether the Industrial Bank of Japan should take the risk on the loan.

This being the 1980s and the bank being Japanese, there was a strong institutional bias in favor of working with Trump, even though he already had a bad reputation as a sleaze who screwed his business partners. But he had currency the Japanese loved: he was famous.

I jammed Trump's figures through Lotus 1-2-3; it wasn't a close call. Even without allowing for the usual *this-is-gonna-be-huuuge* hyperbole common to all real estate developers—not just Trump—and taking the Trump people at their word, there was no way anyone but a total idiot would sign off on such a reckless and foolhardy project. From the start, bankruptcy was written all over this thing. And that's exactly what happened a few years later—without IBJ.

I informed my boss of my findings. He trusted me but was a diligent man, so we drove down to Atlantic City to check out the site. Atlantic City isn't gorgeous now, but at the time it was a war zone.

"Where," I remember asking my boss, "are people supposed to park their cars?"

We weren't going to leave our vehicle on those streets—and the Trump plan we saw didn't include a parking deck.

When we returned to New York, a scowling and characteristically brusque Trump, along with a few of his executives, traipsed over to our office to hear the bad news in person. I remember thinking his suit was too tight.

"Mr. Ted says your numbers don't make sense," explained my boss.

"Who the fuck is Mr. Ted?" Trump asked, looking at me, which I found confusing.

"Who the fuck Mr. Ted is," my boss replied, "is who the fuck says you don't get the fucking money." Best boss ever.

Exit Trump, plus posse, stage right.

He knew we were saying no. Why did he bother to walk over from Trump Tower? I think he wanted to look us in the eye to see who would dare reject him.

I respected that, even though the Taj really was a piece of shit project that insulted us merely by being asked to consider it.

I knew Donald Trump would be a force to be reckoned with for a long time. I just didn't know that he would eventually become a national tragedy or, more precisely, the symptom of one: America's well-documented, long-standing, and constantly worsening anti-intellectualism.

When Democratic presidential nominee Hillary Clinton referred to many of Donald Trump's supporters as a "basket of deplorables," I remarked in a cartoon on the linguistic oddness of the phrase. Matthew Yglesias wrote in *Vox*:

> *Actual English-language use of "deplorables" as a term for a group of people, however, is quite rare, though [Ben] Zimmer [language columnist for The Wall Street Journal] did find Thomas Carlyle in 1831 writing that "of all the deplorables and despicables of this city and time the saddest are the 'literary men.'"*

I have traveled all over the country and talked to Americans from many places, but never I have heard anyone use the word "deplorable" as a noun, much less in the plural. Where the hell was Hillary from? Was she a foreign agent out to infiltrate the White House on behalf of some alien force?

Adding the "basket of" to the word made this soon-to-be iconic phrase sail over the left-field fence into political immortality; her comment turned out to have long, long legs.

Many of Trump's supporters were, in fact, deplorable racists—and not just racist in the typically American quiet way but in a really loud pre-civil rights movement kind of KKK/Nazi way. This white supremacy was seen all too soon when the allied groups of the "alt-right" gathered for a hundreds-strong hate-in in Charlottesville, Virginia. One bigot took the message to its next logical level by driving his car into a crowd of anti-fascist activists, killing a peaceful marcher and injuring several others.

Among the new generation of Republicans, the Trumpists were not just sexists but hard-core misogynists—and not just nationalists but 19th century-style nativists. Bigotry was back, and it was big, boisterous, and proud.

Coastal media outlets didn't have a clue. Where, exactly, did these deplorables come from? Could there really be so many millions of them that they could tip a presidential election away from a well-funded, universally-backed elite like Clinton to a WWE carnival barker like Trump?

Yes, there could be—and were.

But the pundits didn't have a clue. Chastened by the election results, *New York Times* columnists Tom Friedman (just left of center) and David Brooks (just right of center) each announced their plans to go on red-state listening tours in order to escape their bubbles. No word yet on whether they ever made it west of the Hudson River. But their gesture was more than most of their peers offered.

In short order media elite types declared that the 2016 election was not an upset victory by long-simmering forces of reaction that had been there all along, railing against a brand of smug corporate politics hated by just about everyone who didn't live in Manhattan or Silicon Valley. They declared it an anomaly, a perfect storm in which Murphy's Law had run wild: Russian hackers! WikiLeaks! James Comey! Bernie Sanders (somehow, even though he'd campaigned for Hillary)! No one, it seemed, actually wanted to get out there and meet the real people who'd made their voices heard at the ballot box.

So when Harmon told me he planned to get to the bottom of the events leading up to the rise of the Trump phenomenon and The Donald's 2016 election victory, I knew, immediately, that I wanted to be a part of it.

Now that this book exists, people will continue to say they don't understand what happened. But that's because they don't want to know.

The truth is scary.

And thanks to Harmon, it's also hilarious.

–**Ted Rall**

PREFACE

WHERE OTHERS NOT DARE

DONALD J. TRUMP'S IMPROBABLE trek to the White House was characterized by a long and bitter campaign that revealed amongst his followers a joyful support for what we had hoped were relics of America's dark underbelly: racism, sexism, homophobia, Islamophobia, and xenophobia.

During campaign rallies, Trump served as the ringmaster of his own hate-mongering circus, declaiming that "we don't have time to be politically correct." His divided whites against people of color, men against women, straights against gays, Christians against Muslims, and "real" Americans against foreigners (or, more specifically, non-white immigrants).

Due in no small part to Trump's win, we now see a rise of extremist alt-right groups—led by Klansmen and neo-Nazis—and, as a result, are witnessing an increase in hate crimes, anti-immigration sentiment, and mass shootings.

Who were *these* people that Hillary Clinton called "deplorables?"

Were they the same folks that put on *Make America Great Again* hats and filled arenas by the thousands in support of Trump?

Surely, not all of his supporters were one-dimensional racist rednecks who feared government overreach and goose-stepped the streets of America in khaki pants and white polos while carrying tiki torches, waving neo-Nazi flags, and chanting "blood and soil."

Maybe some of his fans simply loved him because of his highly-rated TV show *The Apprentice*? Or others because they were pro-life and he'd promised not only to defund Planned Parenthood but also overturn Roe v. Wade?

What lured me into this exploration of the Trump phenomenon was the manner in which he directly interacted with his supporters on the campaign trail. I wondered what these people saw in him that I didn't.

So, in January 2016 I signed up for The Donald's campaign email list, where his rise to power was narrated through the daily messages sent to his most devout followers. As he painted his view of the world through Trump-colored glasses, the trajectory of those emails devolved from an initially confident and arrogant self-funded candidate to a desperate crackpot pleading for campaign donations.

At first, the rhetorical strategy of Trump's emails employed an almost humble approach, carving out an optimistic John F. Kennedy better-tomorrow-style. Lifting the "silent majority" line from Nixon and "Make America Great Again" from Reagan, Trump's tone was positive:

> *The silent majority is no longer silent. We will no longer be led by the all talk, no action politicians that have failed us all. Together, we are going to Make America Great Again.*

Soon, with the campaign running low on funds, his emails took a different tone, offering perks such as the Donald Trump Black Card—which had no intrinsic value—for top contributors:

> *I want to commemorate those patriotic men and women who made a contribution during this critical time ... Carriers of TRUMP Black Cards will be remembered for never giving up, never turning their back during the final stretch of our campaign ... only Black Card members can claim to have been there until the very end.*

Trump's campaign treated these emails as if they were a pitch for his fraudulent Trump University, which wasn't surprising. Many of us knew that Trump would say whatever necessary to appease his loyal supporters and raise money for his campaign.

Unsatisfied with reading email propaganda from home and sitting on the sidelines as an observer, it was time to throw myself directly into the eye of the *deplorable* storm and rub shoulders with the flesh-and-blood people that many Americans will never have a chance to meet face-to-face.

My mission was simple: take a quixotic journey deep into the heart of Trump America and hold up a mirror to modern conservative life in an attempt to understand—by posing as a right-wing conservative—the motivations, desires, and actions of the deplorables who helped elect him.

This was nothing new for me. I have made a career out of infiltrating extremist groups, putting my neck on the line for the sake of knowledge and satire. While other writers have endeavored to analyze the Trump phenomenon, none (to my knowledge) has attempted my Margaret Mead-like approach, where I typically alter my look, attitude, and locale, venturing where others not dare in order to harvest illuminating, shocking, and just plain bizarre results by chasing answers to the difficult questions most journalists aren't asking.

What is the thought process behind a Texas gun store owner who labeled his establishment a ***Muslim Free Zone***? What motivates a New Hampshire man to get a likeness of Donald Trump tattooed across his chest? What actually happens in a Christian conversion therapy group? How does it feel to canvass for Trump on the campaign trail and knock on strangers' doors? What do anti-immigration groups really do to repel immigrants at the border?

I attempt to answer those questions—and more—in the pages that follow: a weird, anthropological romp into how red state voters live ... and think. **So, let's put on our *Make America Great Again* hats and meet the deplorables ...**

–Harmon Leon

PURE CRAZY TRUMP FANATICS

PART ONE

INTRODUCTION

AMERICANS ARE STUPID. SO WHAT?

THIS IS HOW STUPID AMERICANS ARE

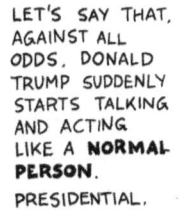

ELECTION DAY 2016 SHOCKED the world and at least half the United States. Even with the archaic Electoral College—and Hillary Clinton's lackluster campaign—how could it be that close to fifty percent of the electorate of the world's oldest democracy could have chosen to hand Donald Trump control of the nuclear launch codes?

Donald Trump was famous. Some might even call him notorious. He had name recognition and an animal cunning—for how to churn up long-ignored resentments and transmogrify them into a new-fangled populist-fueled electoral victory—that the Clinton campaign didn't have.

But he had at least as much going against him. He was physically unappealing in an age of television. He had never run for political office of any kind. He didn't offer a single specific policy prescription. And he said one outrageous thing after another, not a few of which ought to have offended the Republican voters he was courting, such as insulting Senator John McCain for getting captured by the North Vietnamese. Yet he won.

How did that happen?

We shouldn't have been that surprised, because the same thing had happened twelve years earlier, when Americans voted for a president they knew with absolute certainty to be an idiot. In 2004 American's voted to reelect George W. Bush by a sizable margin. This was almost two years after Bush lied America into war against Iraq. By that time, even the Bush Administration had admitted there were never any weapons of mass destruction in Iraq.

John Kerry, Bush's Democratic challenger, had been on both right sides of Vietnam history: he volunteered and served heroically. Then he came home to attest that the war was a mistake, immoral, and a looming disaster.

It was an easy choice, and Americans made it. As the headline of the UK newspaper *The Daily Mirror* asked the morning after election day, "How can 59,054,087 people be so DUMB?"

Yeah, well, we're a dumb people.

That's what people say. Especially foreigner, non-American people.

But lots of Americans think that Americans are stupid—not them, of course. They think other Americans are stupid.

It will not, even if you're an idiot, come as a shock when I admit here that one of the Americans who think Americans are intellectually challenged is me.

Moronitude exists everywhere, of course. What makes stupidity in America stand out is that most Americans—the dumb ones—don't think it's bad to be dumb. Far from being ashamed, they're dumb and proud. To the contrary, the dumb ones make fun of the small-and-constantly-shrinking population of intelligent ones: the "nerds."

Want to study astrophysics? You're a geek. No prom date for you!

I haven't been everywhere, but I've traveled a lot, and what historians have documented as the tradition of anti-intellectualism in America seems to be pretty unique. Even Australia, land of our cultural Anglo-Saxon brethren, where dwarf-tossing was a thing (and for all I know may still be), never had an actual political party called the Know Nothings. We did, and not only that, when historians reference the Know Nothings, no one ever chortles in derision. They nod knowingly. Maybe.

Flat affect. That's what we do.

From *The Simpsons* to Green Day's punk rock opera *American Idiot* to the semi-banned Mike Judge movie *Idiocracy*, our cultural commentators have taken repeated stabs at our "dumb and proud" national attitude. Yet it doesn't change.

This, after all, is a country in which smart people have to pretend—in the words of an '80s song by Flipper—to "act stupider than you really are" in order to fit in.

Reality TV and televangelists aside, nothing epitomizes the national cult of stultification more clearly than our electoral politics. On the Republican side, well-read men and women of considerable accomplishment and with impressive educational credentials that belie what I am about to describe find themselves pretending to believe in things they and everyone else with half a brain can't possibly believe to be true—because so many of the voters they need are just that damned stupid.

This is how we get actual United States Senator Ted Cruz, no dummy he, at least not according to the guys who lost repeated college debates to him, pretending not to believe that climate change is caused by humans. Not to mention a bunch of governors and senators—senators!—claiming to believe in "God" and a six thousand-year-old Earth because of the Bible.

A friend who hung out with George W. Bush told me something I've heard often enough to almost believe: the guy is actually intelligent.

In a way this comes as a relief, because: launch codes (also Yale and Harvard). Even a legacy admit to Ivy League institutions shouldn't be half as much of the colossal idiot brush-clearing hick Bush pretended to be his entire political life.

There were hints of Bush's non-stupidity. Every now and then, his aw-shucks cornpone veneer would flake off and the Connecticut Yankee inflection of a grandson of Prescott Bush would peek out like the cobblestones and streetcar tracks of an old paved-over road after a hard winter. That stupid accent—all fake!

It reminded me of something Bush biographer Kitty Kelly reported: after losing a local election in Texas, Dubya swore, Scarlet-like, never to get out-countrified again. And he didn't. And it worked.

How depressing.

Given how much I beat up Generalissimo El Busho while he was bombing and Gitmo-ing and bank-bailing, it's only fair that I point out: he's one of many. Obama and Hillary both applied a reverseclassist downscaling filter to their locutions, and Jesus H. W. Christ, it's so over-the-top phony. Am I the only one who can tell?

Speaking of which, I attribute the 2016 Bernie Sanders-Donald Trump surge to the two outsiders' surprisingly unscripted authenticity (or, in Trump's case, the appearance thereof), part of which derives from their unspun, startling, old-school New York accents. Platform planks took a back seat to reality, which says something.

Not that these two mavericks of right and left weren't forced to breathe the sludgy water of stupidism through their previously pure gills.

The Donald and The Bern: both men are smart (despite the former insisting on saying it about himself, it happens to be true). Notwithstanding *The Apprentice* and the Ivana mess, Trump had to dumb himself down still further (i.e., the **Make America Great Again** baseball cap). The socialist senator from Vermont refrained from talking American, which is why he didn't bother to campaign in the South. So many pundits, so few who enjoy a Marx-inflected class analysis.

Burying the lede as much as I possibly can— in a nation where the life of the mind is valued, this is not considered a vice—this brings us to: why?

Why are we dumb and proud?

I blame our schools. We learn facts but not how to think. Rhetoric, debate, logical reasoning are optional after-school activities. So we grow up believing that everyone is entitled to their opinion, each as valid as any other, even though this cannot possibly be true.

But I could be wrong.

–**Ted Rall**

Now, journey with **Harmon** into *real* America, the land of the "dumb and proud," as he infiltrates some pure crazy Trump fanatics ...

CHAPTER 1

TRUMP: THE ROCK & ROLL MUSE

POLITICAL MOVEMENTS ENCOMPASS A variety of strategies and activities: canvassing for voters, putting up yard signs, crunching data, writing letters to the editor, chatting with the neighbors. Some people might look at a call center and say, "That's not for me ... but there must something I can do to help my candidate prevail at the polls." They offer their skills, whatever they may be, to the cause.

Sometimes those skills are a little off-beat. But that doesn't mean they don't have an effect, if for no other reason but to showcase devotion to the cause.

Touched by the Trump muse, singer-songwriter Nathan Olivarez formed the hard-rocking band Brothers N Arms, which in December 2016 released its first single: "Trump for America."

Olivarez, who looks exactly like the kind of *bad hombre* Trump wants to deport, and his brother Jacob have been playing music together for the past fifteen years. "I've never done a political song," he admitted. The duo, based in Bakersfield, California, charted a new musical course after attending a Donald Trump rally.

"When we heard Trump speak, we said, 'Hey, we're going to back this candidate up,'" Olivarez said. "This thing is going to be a movement. We have to do something!"

Inspired by Trump's words, Olivarez decided to write his first political anthem: "I felt I could make a patriotic song just for Trump ... I have six albums, and I've probably written over sixty songs. With my musical talent, I wanted to give what I could to the movement. I wanted to give a song that they could use to rally people ... I felt like I had to help out and get the message out there—and that was it."

The Olivarez siblings started Brothers N Arms as a side project to their Slipknot-esqe band, State Of Insomnia, which has opened for metal acts Disturbed and Static-X.

"It's a whole different genre, yeah," said Olivarez, whose musical focus shifted to "support Donald Trump, Second Amendment rights, and all that is America," according to the album notes. "I've never been political. I don't believe in mixing politics with music, but this is actually created for Trump."

Olivarez cranked out the anthem "Trump for America" in no time. "I wanted to capture a feeling," he said. "I thought, 'Wow, this guy is going to be real.' It's kind of refreshing. Let's go by that feeling of America."

The last time Olivarez voted was in 1996: for Bill Clinton. "I used to be a Democrat—hardcore," he admitted.

But then he grew tired of politicians, unhappy with a portion of the Republican Party, and wanted somebody new to bring change. "Trump is kind of a savior. Trump is the only man that will bring Democrats and Republicans and Independents together. There's not one other candidate that will do it," he argued, predicting Trump's bipartisan and unifying power.

Oh well.

It may be true that hindsight is twenty-twenty, but in this case, so was foresight. Beginning with his fiery inaugural address, Trump seemed determined to govern and speak from the far right, and the divisiveness only worsened after that.

"He's the only one who talks about the things that we all think ... about the political correctness and things like that," said Olivarez, who also professed that he saw Trump as a "down-to-earth, authentic man" and a "blue-collar billionaire."

Olivarez recalled what it was like growing up in Texas: "We were always proud Americans. I feel like people lost that. I really didn't write the song with intentions on how it was going to turn out. I just kind of went with my feelings."

Ultimately, he felt that Trump just wanted to give back to Americans. "He's frustrated with the government and all the corruptness," Olivarez said. "I feel Trump is like my grandfather who would give me good advice, even though it's not sugar-coated."

The Olivarez brothers posted the "Trump for America" video to YouTube, where it has been viewed over one hundred thousand times.

"This kind of took off by accident. I just went by feeling, and I did something cool. I just felt I needed to do my part," Olivarez said. "For us, it's good. It's only a single release. I just kind of released it because of Trump—and it's already getting quite hyped."

"Trump for America" was picked up by conservative radio shows and covered by the local news. Just as it went viral on Twitter, the Right Side Broadcasting Network began playing it before every Trump rally.

"When you're a musician and you write a song—and you first hear it—you're your own kind of critic," said Olivarez. "It stuck in my own head. Would I like this song if it were somebody else that wrote it? To me, it was really catchy."

The chorus of "Trump for America" goes:

> ***Believe in America***
> ***Fight for America***
> ***Change for America***
> ***Trump for America***

"It's a pro-America song," Olivarez explained, in case there was any confusion. "When you look at the concept of the video, it's like everybody coming together and making a change in America. It's kind of like saying, 'We're done with the politics. Let's start making things happen.'"

The "Trump for America" video ticks all the boxes of a right-wing checklist of patriotic clichés: 9/11 firemen (check); kids reciting the Pledge of Allegiance (check); troops, a baseball game, monster trucks, and John Wayne, (check). Not since Hulk Hogan's video for "Real American" has there been such a red, white, and blue-gasm of nationalism. The Olivarez video was so patriotic that it makes you want to fuck a cheeseburger while watching *Top Gun*.

"It's a family-based song. That's why I have the kids reciting the Pledge of Allegiance in the middle," he said, explaining the nuances. "I didn't write it to be cool. I wrote it because of a feeling. I figure people could hum it, and your kids could listen to it. And it was just a good friendly patriotic song."

Asked to theorize about the support his Trump anthem has received from fans, Olivarez replied, "Maybe people are hopeful of change. They want something new, and I feel like it's an inspiring song for hope."

The song's YouTube comments echo the sentiments of the Trump movement:

This song reminds you of a country when the people were true Americans and proud of it!!!

Pro-America propaganda. About damn time.

God bless you!! Yes ... Trump for America! Thank you so much for this awesome song! Trump is that hope and last chance!

This song makes my dick hard meanwhile making left wing nutcases cry.

"My old fans don't even know that I'm in this band doing this. I've never really done anything political, so my fan base is all different now," Olivarez said. "It's kind of a mix. They really love the music, but at the same time, they're Trump supporters."

Olivarez received supportive messages from people in other countries, which he found weird. They said things like: "I'm not even American, and I love this song. I hope you elect Trump."

But the real surprise comes from those closer to home. "I get veterans who tell me that the song makes them cry. I didn't expect to get those kind of comments," Olivarez said. "It's almost flattering. But at the same time, it's almost like, 'Wow!' I'm just kind of in shock. I'm proud of it. But at the same time, it's humbled me even more. I feel good like I contributed—if that makes any sense."

Quicker than you could say, "The Donald stole Ronald Reagan's

Make America Great slogan," pro-Trump songs, during the 2016 election season, became a niche genre onto itself. Musically speaking, Olivarez believed "Trump for America" was head-and-shoulders above his patriotic Trump anthem competition. "There are a couple of songs out there I'm not too impressed with," he sniped. "They didn't have the feeling like my song has. They're not as inspiring."

After listening to the "competition," I saw his point. In one such entry, Team America met free-styling, including a pumped-up chorus about building a wall on the border and sending Mexico the bill.

The Trump songs were easy to spot: they were usually titled with some variation of his campaign slogan. For example, take "Make America Great Again," which shouldn't be confused with the song "Make America Great Again."

"I heard a couple of rap songs for Trump, and I was never that impressed," Olivarez said.

What!? How could he not be impressed with the rap "Pump the Trump," which featured all the musical finesse of two white guys rapping in a McDonald's Happy Meal commercial?

Olivarez wasn't a fan of the "Official Donald Trump Jam" as well. "I have heard that song," he said. "I wasn't very impressed with that either."

"The Official Donald Trump Jam," featuring the red, white, and blue-clad USA Freedom Kids—who ended up suing the Trump campaign for lack of payment relating to their appearances—captured what every Saturday night would feel like if Nazi Germany had won the war.

Regarding Brothers N Arms' new musical direction, Olivarez said, "We're getting other music together. I am looking at other patriotic songs. This is kind of a pro-America band." He claimed that they could be like Pink Floyd and release an entire Trump concept album, which would also be called, you know ... *The Wall*.

The band has already planned a second version of "Trump for America." "I thought, 'Why don't we just put "God Bless America" through the whole thing and take the Trump part out,' just in case the song took off," said Olivarez. "One day, somebody might want to play it at school. It's an American anthem."

While Olivarez saw his song as an anthem for all Americans, others were not as amused: "Oh, of course. You always get haters." And these haters love to leave comments on YouTube, including:

This has to be a South Park sketch ... okay Matt and Trey, come out anytime now.

Honestly thought this was a joke song at first. Clearly you stand behind it and a lot ... a LOT of people like it. Personally, I think this is the biggest hunk of crap I've ever heard. I wish there were a way I could emphasize how incredibly terrible this song is ...

The typical hater comment was seldom directed at the song and more towards Trump. "Oh, that he's racist," Olivarez explained, before adding: "Typical uneducated things."

In his other YouTube videos, Olivarez, while looking directly at the camera, echoed Trump's tough policies on immigration, suggesting automatic prison time for undocumented immigrants who wave the flag of another country.

"I don't understand that. Wouldn't you be waving the American flag? Isn't that the country you want to stay in and belong in? To me," Olivarez reasoned, "it's like being a Raiders fan, walking into the Raiders' stadium, but I'm going to wave a Denver Broncos flag! You wouldn't do it in sports. Why would you do it for your country? I mean, it doesn't make any sense."

Actually, it makes perfect sense. But since I was there to observe this part of the ecosystem, not change it, I didn't have the heart to tell Olivarez that the premise of his analogy was flawed. If the Raiders' stadium represented America, then the stadium was filled with fans of possibly many teams. These fans were free to wave whichever flag they chose, whether it be a Raiders flag, a Broncos flag, or a Rainbow flag. Therefore, it is quite possible that a Broncos fan might visit the Raiders' stadium, cheer on his team, and perhaps wave a flag that is not a Broncos flag. This could happen. This does happen. Maybe Olivarez hasn't been to many football games.

Or maybe Olivarez's position regarding flags explains why he believes that the main fountain of hate comments have come from Hispanics. That and this surprising fact: he is "American-Hispanic" (note how he puts the "American" first). For musically supporting the man who wants to build a wall to keep out Mexicans, he has been called "a traitor" and "a Judas."

"I'm five generations American. I don't even have family in Mexico. I am an American," Olivarez said. "I'm the victim of other Hispanics who are uneducated or ignorant and assume because I'm brown I should be sticking with Mexico, when I don't even know anything about Mexico. This is about your country comes first. The only country I'd be a traitor of is America if I did that."

The accusations made Olivarez laugh. "To me, I don't even know what I'm a traitor of," he said. "When you're illegal and you know you're breaking the law and you're upset that someone wants you to obey the law—I don't understand it."

Olivarez equated allowing illegal immigrants into the county with driving drunk. "It's like saying to every DUI person, 'Okay, keep drinking and driving. We're okay with it. It's fine.'"

While this thought process about immigrants seems illogical to many people, he reasoned: "If these guys can do it, then why can't people drive drunk? It's illegal, too, but just let it slide."

According to Olivarez, Trump has been misunderstood by the media and a majority of Americans. "I really have never heard anything that Trump has said that is racist," he affirmed. "I'm only defending myself half the time when people find out I'm Hispanic and say things like, 'Oh, I can't believe you would write a song for that racist.'"

Laughing, he added, "It's like he's not even racist. To me, it's like saying I'm racist. But I'm not racist. I don't understand. I don't comprehend it."

Brothers N Arms claimed that their "Trump for America" anthem wasn't meant to divide people. "I don't want this song to be a message against any race or anything," Olivarez proclaimed. "I think, if anything, my song talks about uniting all national origins—and really this feeling of all to stand united."

What if Trump hadn't received the Republican nomination? Would Olivarez have voted for another candidate?

"Nope! Me—and pretty much every follower I have—pledged not to support anyone else," he admitted. For Trump supporters to back anybody else would have been "going against what we believe."

For Olivarez, it was Trump all the way to the White House—or bust. "The movement is all or nothing. That's why I wrote the song," he said. "The only way we can disrupt Washington is with an outsider. An ordinary man has to go in … and there's never been a billionaire guy who has been authentic that would ever run for office."

A few months prior to the election, Brothers N Arms and Olivarez were still waiting for word about an important gig from the big guy upstairs: no, not Jesus—Trump!

"I'm only performing at this point if Trump asks me to," Olivarez said.

But a great wall existed between Olivarez and his dream. "I have not heard anything from Trump himself or any of his people. I'd like to be the headliner to be honest," he said with optimism. "Other than that, if he asks me to play, I'll go play."

Trump didn't ask. But there's always 2020.

CHAPTER 2

INK ME SOME TRUMP

MANY, IF NOT MOST, Americans believe that the human body was created by God in His image. It's precious real estate: the average person only has around eighteen square feet of skin. Whether one favors a tramp stamp, a full sleeve, or a complete body suit like Ray Bradbury's character the Illustrated Man, they want to think long and hard about a decision that—tattoo removal services aside—can never be taken back completely. A tattoo is for life.

Since the political tattoo is perhaps the most ephemeral of all tattoos, I wanted to know what kind of people were so dedicated to supporting Donald Trump that they would carve his image onto their skin for time immemorial—or at least until they lay mouldering in their grave.

The very day after Trump won the crucial New Hampshire primary, I was en route to the small town of Seabrook and Clay Dragon Tattoo, sandwiched between a Church of Christ and a store advertising Totally Nude Ladies. The parlor's proprietor, Bob Holmes, made worldwide news when—to show his support for Donald Trump—he offered free tattoos of the loudmouth presidential candidate. As they say in New Hampshire, Live Free or Die ... or Look Stupid Trying.

"I have little old ladies calling me up and crying and telling me, 'God Bless You!'" Holmes said of his bold act of political immortality.

A veteran tattoo artist with thirty-two years of experience, Holmes administered forty-one free Trump tattoos over a couple of weeks during early 2016—and the numbers grew daily throughout the campaign. Earlier this week, a mother and daughter came in to the shop and each asked to have Trump's **Make America Great Again** slogan tattooed across their chests.

"They're doing the slogan. They're doing the Trump head. They're doing customized flags. They're doing so many different kinds of things. We're not limited," Holmes said. "Have you ever seen the Donald Trump picture of him as Uncle Sam? That, I would LOVE to do!"

The free Trump tattoo frenzy was set off after Holmes made an off-the-cuff remark to a British reporter. When asked if he'd ever done a Donald Trump tattoo, Holmes replied, "I haven't done any of them, but I'd do them for free." The reporter put that in her article.

Within days, his political ink-quip went viral. Rather than welch on his gibe, Holmes correlated his action to that of his real estate mogul political hero and kept his word. "I'm not the kind of guy who'd open his mouth and not do what I say," Holmes declared as a tattoo gun buzzed in the background.

"I relate to Donald Trump because I think he's mouthy and opinionated—but he stands up for something," said Holmes, who previously had never voted in a single election. But in 2016 he was inspired. "There's no one else out there that could run this country—at all. Everyone just lies, you know."

On the other side of the ideological ink divide, a Vermont tattoo parlor drew political lines (in ink) by offering gratis Bernie Sanders tattoos, which featured a caricature of the democratic socialist's signature glasses and flyover hair. "What does it take, two fucking seconds to do?" Holmes spat as he compared a Bernie tattoo to his carefully crafted Trump tattoo. "That's the difference between a Donald Trump supporter and a Bernie supporter."

No one had entered Holmes' parlor to request a tattoo of any of the other candidates, although Holmes once suggested that a client get a tattoo depicting Trump's foot resting on Hillary Clinton's head. Classy!

"I'm amazed that so many people are getting Donald Trump tattoos," remarked Holmes, who was booked solid for weeks after the news story went viral.

But it's not surprising: some people would drink arsenic if it were offered for free. Still, you have to admire the dedication of a voter willing to make a stand for their candidate that will extend into the distant future, long after car bumper stickers have peeled away, breasts have lost the battle to gravity, and *MAGA* has turned all blue and blurry. Think about it: how many Al Gore tattoos do you see?

Guided by the vague belief that everyone "wants to make America great again and change the way the world is going because we lost our country ... we lost our freedom," Holmes picked *The Apprentice* star, believing that he was the only candidate who could steer the U.S. towards racial harmony, even if it takes building a wall to keep out Mexicans and barring Muslims from entering the country.

"It's become more racist now than it was ten years ago," he said. "We're probably back to the '30s and '40s with racism now—and that was all Obama's doing," he added without a hint of irony or elaboration.

Regarding his own Trump tattoo, Holmes' big dream remained unfulfilled. "I'm waiting for Donald Trump to come here and sign my arm—his signature. Then, I'll have one of my guys tattoo it on me," he said. "If he could come here and do that, then I will have something no one else could have. And I'm all about that."

Prior to my encounter with Holmes, I had never met a Donald Trump supporter; he was my first. As with a St. Pauli Girl (or a herpes outbreak), you never forget your first. And now, here at Clay Dragon in Seabrook, I was about to meet supporters so fanatical that they were willing to permanently ink Donald Trump's face on their bodies. It felt as if Christmas had once again come early.

◆

MEET BILL, A FORTY-SIX-YEAR-OLD military veteran and former Los Angeles police officer. "We haven't had a decent president since Ronald Reagan," he said, providing the rationale, if such a thing were possible, for his *Make America Great Again* tattoo, freshly inked on his left shoulder.

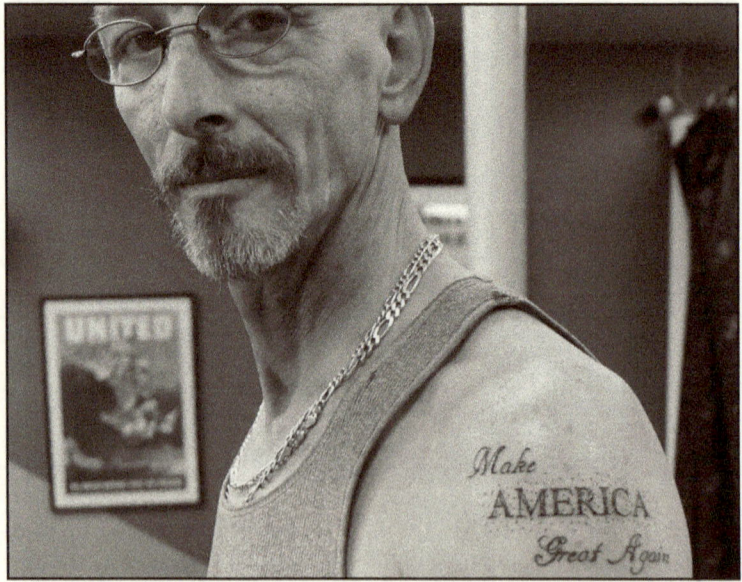

Bearing a slight resemblance to Walter White's Heisenberg alter-ego from *Breaking Bad*, the current constable of Seabrook hadn't voted since the 1980s. And more importantly, it had been five years since receiving his last tattoo.

"This one was the first spur of the moment tattoo. It was something I felt I had to do!" he explained. "You just don't throw pretty pictures on your arm. You get tattoos because they mean something to you. It doesn't matter if it was free or one hundred dollars. It's irrelevant what's the price. So that's kind of why I did it."

Gesturing to the Trump motto on his shoulder, Bill said that it was something he believed in. "Who doesn't want to make America great?" he asked. "We all have the opinion that things have gone to shit!"

Bill, who has known Bob Holmes for years, saw the free Trump tattoo campaign as a political movement. "If Bob felt so strongly about something, then there had to be something to it," he said. "He doesn't take anything light-heartedly. If he got serious about it, then I had to look into it. You know what? I believe in this. I see where he's coming from."

As a devout believer in the movement, Bill even sent an interested person to the shop to talk to Bob: "He just happened to need a canvas, so it worked out well."

Speaking about his support of Trump and Trump tattoos, Bill waxed philosophical: "It takes the two of us to get it started, but if it picks up and millions of people get involved—awesome!"

For Bill, his Trump tattoo was an ideological manifesto. "It's a commitment. You can say you support a candidate. You can say you support an understanding or belief. But to get a tattoo, which is for the rest of your life, that's a commitment," he said. "And that's kind of the statement I wanted to make. I believe in making America great to the point where I'm willing to wear it for the rest of my life. The people I've talked to feel the exact same way!"

He failed, however, to mention the immense federal bureaucracy that would be necessitated by the production of millions of Trump tattoos. Perhaps this enterprise would be the start of the future president's vaunted promise to **Make America Great Again** by rebuilding the nation's crumbling graphic arts infrastructure—one tattoo at a time.

"So the tattoo is kind of a way to show people our commitment, not just to Donald Trump but the idea that we want to make America great again. He coined the phrase," claimed Bill. "And I'm going to pick it up and carry it—for the rest of my life!"

Actually, the slogan was first used by Ronald Reagan's 1980 campaign. Still, Bill determined that it was necessary for everyone to get behind the phrase. "It's not just Trump who is going to make America great. It's everybody. He's the spearhead; we're the arrow behind it," he said, deploying a classic archery metaphor. "We see a hope where there hasn't been any for so long ... So that's why I got the tattoo. I believe in what it stands for!"

Bill's sibling, a Democrat, disagreed with the decision. "My brother said, 'Hopefully, tattoo removals are free.' I said, 'Why? I'm not going to get this removed regardless.'

"It's not just because of Donald Trump. He started this and gave us the verbiage. He's just making it easy for us to get that point out. It's turned into a movement, but all good things start at some point."

Of course, all bad things begin at some point, too.

◆

Meet Dmitri, a twenty-four-year-old ex-felon (or once a felon always a felon, depending on your point of view). He gave up crime to work at a pizza place.

"I saw the free Trump tattoos on the news. Called that night. You know, just impulse," said Dmitri, a manic guy covered in jailhouse tattoos. His friends drove him two hours from Cape Cod so that he could get his free Trump tattoo. "When I called, they said, 'Do you want the slogan?' No, I want the face!"

Dmitri explained why he wanted Trump's likeness permanently placed on his body. "It's a story for me. Like ten years from now, 'Yeah—this dude ran for president,'" he said. "If he became president, that's one thing. Right? That'd be awesome.

"But if he became president ... and got assassinated ... that's another story right there. Right? Like, 'Dude, dead president on my leg!' So this is good. Win-win. And win-win-win, because it's ink on my body for free!"

Self-aware to a fault, Dmitri realized that not everyone loves the idea of a Trump tattoo. "Ah, my mother hates it. She thinks Donald Trump is ignorant and hates everybody," he said, explaining that she was a Hillary supporter. "I have no idea honestly. I don't even care who is president at all. Period! It's just a story for me."

With that said, before going under the ink, Dmitri conferred with Holmes about his idea for a Trump tattoo.

"If I were a jujitsu guy, I'd put Donald Trump on my thigh. So, right before I KO a guy, that's what he'd see," he said while demonstrating exactly how he would accomplish this feat.

Dmitri, unfortunately, was not a jujitsu master. Instead, he brainstormed how to improve the Trump portrait slated for his calf. "What do you think of adding the Trump Towers in the background?" he inquired. "That would be cool!"

Discussion erupted as to whether the backdrop should be the Trump Towers—which would be difficult since there currently is only one original Trump Tower on Fifth Avenue in New York—or, instead, a 9/11 motif with the late Twin Towers of the World Trade Center. Finally, compromise was too difficult: no architecture. Trump's face and an American Flag prevailed.

But Dmitri was not done. "How cool would it be if we did dollar signs instead of stars on the flag? Just improvise the dollar signs," he suggested. "I don't care about those. Throw that in there!"

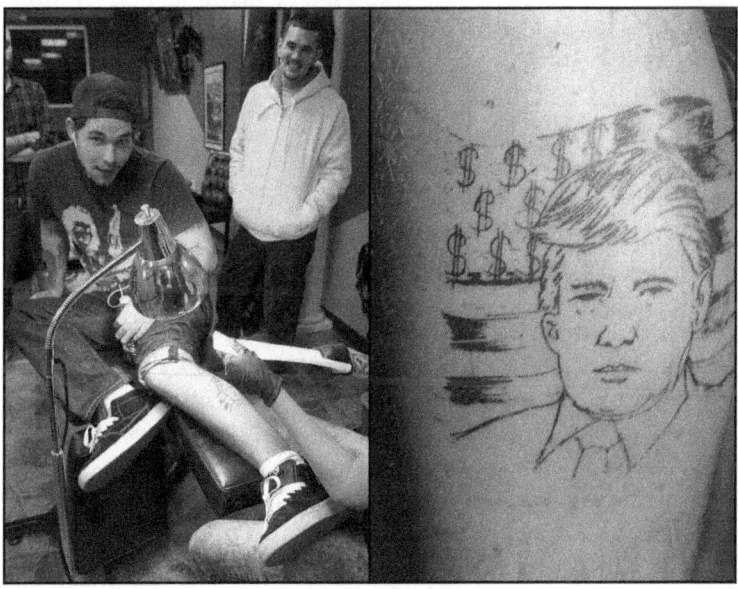

Not wanting to be outdone, Holmes joined the playful banter. "So, if I wanted to add Hillary Clinton on a chain collar with a ball gag over here, that would be okay?" he joked, before adding, "'Cause that's where that bitch oughta go!"

After the inking, Dmitri had nothing but fanboy adulation for his new Trump tattoo, which would complement his next planned tattoo: an angel and demon holding guns and a machete. "I love it. I love the fact that it has the money signs in there," he said. "I love that it was free. I love that I had an awesome tattoo artist do it. It just came out on point."

Even though Dmitri was inked with Trump for life, he admitted that he wouldn't vote for the candidate: "Me? No. I'm a felon. I can't vote."

◆

Meet Max, a twenty-six-year-old construction worker from across the Massachusetts state line. "I support Trump, man. You know," he said in a gravelly voice. Max had returned to the shop for more inking.

"I did the portrait like a week ago. It took maybe an hour. It wasn't too bad," he explained about Trump's face, which had recently been inked on his calf. "I've been to Bob's shop before. I knew about it. I was willing to do it. Up and did it."

Max pulled up his pant leg, revealing the portrait of Trump's head, which vaguely resembled the Gerber Baby, surrounded by the words ***Make America Great Again***.

"There's a lot more you can do to it. Who knows, I might add some more. But I support Trump," he said, pointing to the tattoo. "He's behind me, and I'm behind him … literally."

Even if Trump had lost, Max was committed to displaying Trump's face on his body for the rest of his life. "He's an icon. It's pop culture. He's been around my entire childhood," Max said. "I mean, he's a pretty popular guy. He just breathes success. You know what I mean? He's a successful guy—someone to look towards and to shoot for. So I think it's cool. It is what it is."

So true, as it would be difficult to live in a world that isn't "what it is."

Max, who had only voted in one previous election, said that he wouldn't consider a tattoo of any other politician. "I really don't trust any other candidates. I can relate to Trump," he said. "I agree with a lot of what he's saying.

"I'm a working dad, working class. So, I support him—and what he believes in—and trust what he says. The past election, I didn't have kids, and now I have kids. So, I'm looking towards the future. It's all about my future and the kids' future. If he's not in it, then I'm not voting."

Photos of Max's Gerber Baby Trump tattoo, which he posted to Facebook, received mixed reactions. "All the people I know, who don't do anything all day—they live off the government … just sit on their ass and do nothing—they all hate it," Max said. "Everyone that's a construction worker—a hard worker working forty plus hours a week—were like, 'Ah man, that's epic! I love it!' I think that shows a lot right there."

◆

MEET CODY, A TWENTY-FOUR-YEAR-OLD construction worker who was contemplating a free Trump tattoo. "I saw it, and people were talking about it," he said. "And I was like, 'Yay.' Then I was saying, 'No.' Then I said, 'Screw it—why not?'"

If Cody decided to go through with it, then Holmes, that very afternoon, would have been challenged with his most elaborate Trump tattoo to date. His assistant, Heather, drew up Cody's potential tattoo: Donald Trump standing in front of an American flag, ripping open his shirt, and exposing a Superman logo underneath.

"That's sick!" Cody exclaimed as the Trump/Superman sketch evolved. "I would defiantly go with that."

Equally as excited, Holmes added, "That's your Trump Stamp right there. That's what they're calling it now, worldwide. They're calling it Trump Stamps."

For nearly a month, Cody had been thinking about adding a Trump tattoo to compliment the Forever Young ink on his chest. "It's just something crazy. I didn't know what to get," he said. "I have a couple of pieces I'm waiting to get, and I wanted another tattoo."

And for Cody, it didn't matter if Trump were to lose the race. He said the tattoo, like all great *art*, would take on a different meaning years in the future: "I'm going to think back to the crazy memories I had here, and I'm going to love every minute of them."

Cody's friends, also Trump supporters, couldn't wait to see his new tattoo, which possibly impacted his decision to proceed. Now ready to go for the gusto, he told Holmes, "If you really want to, you can do a chest piece. You're doing it. It's up to you. Go wild now. I don't care. I just want a tattoo, and this is going to be big!"

Finally, Cody took his place in the tattoo chair. After the Trump/Superman stencil was applied, the inking process commenced. Cody winced in pain. His body involuntarily twitched, distracting Holmes' concentration and the precision movements of his tattoo gun.

"Are you done moving?" Holmes asked Cody while trying to concentrate on the lines around Trump's hair. "Good, 'cause I'm doing his face. Normally, I wouldn't care, but it's Donald Trump."

As Holmes continued, Cody kept twitching and wincing, almost to the point where it seemed as if he were being subjected to a forced Bernie tattoo.

"It's whether you want a Donald Trump tattoo or end up having it look like frickin' Hillary," Holmes warned his wimpy, non-paying customer. "It doesn't matter if it hurts him. Because in the end, he's getting a good piece of artwork."

While focusing on the colors of Trump's Superman shirt, Holmes explained the nuances of a good Trump tattoo. "It's all just shading to get the look you want. If you do the eyes wrong, you're not going to get the facial features you want," he said.

"Yeah, he'll look like a chink," Cody blurted out while wincing once again as the tattoo gun continued to carve Trump's likeness into his flesh. "It's going to be worth it in the end," he added.

Cody, still enduring pain, looked down at Trump's smiling face, now permanently inked on his body. Yet his loyalty to Trump transcended the tattoo. "He's very outspoken, and he speaks his mind. And that's what I like about him," he said. "That, and I don't like Bernie Sanders!"

CHAPTER 3

KNOCKING ON DOORS FOR TRUMP

I FOUND MYSELF STANDING on the stoop of a stranger's house in an affluent suburban Philadelphia neighborhood holding a stack of Donald Trump for President flyers and a clipboard—to make me look official. I was hoping that said stranger would not answer the door.

"Doorbells aren't reliable. So, I always knock," explained my trainer, evidently a victim of ringless doorbells. Earlier, we had shared a laugh about "lying and crooked" Hillary. Now, I prayed the wind wouldn't blow off my oversized **Make America Great Again** hat that matched the colorful golf shirt I was wearing—my Republican disguise—thus exposing my liberal-loving dreadlocks and my true identity.

Seconds after knocking, an annoyed man popped his head out the door. I heard myself gushing over the merits of Donald Trump's beautiful, beautiful wall—a big, solid brick and mortar structure visible from outer space—that he was promising to build on the Mexican border.

"Can I leave you some literature?" I asked. My victim did not reply. When I tried handing him a *Make America Great Again* flyer, blazoned with a confident Trump giving a thumbs-up, the door was slammed in my face. I had encountered another America-hater.

"That happens a lot," said my trainer. "That's nothing personal. That's just someone who doesn't like Republicans." I vigorously nodded my head.

It was July 9, 2016, many long months before Trump would shock the political journosphere and cover Nate Silver with shame everlasting as a result of his shocking election victory. I was undercover as a Trump campaign volunteer, going door-to-door and canvassing on Trump's National Day of Training. This ordeal wasn't my Dante purgatory moment, nor had I been sentenced for crimes against Bernie. Months before, I went online and added my name to Donald Trump's email list.

Then, after receiving an urgent campaign message with a very subtle subject line (*Help Mr. Trump Beat Crooked Hillary!*), I decided that it was time to rub elbows with Trump volunteers by becoming one of them. Nothing provides insight into the rise of a political movement like observing the unique perspective of those who campaign for its victory from the very start.

Like the plebes who flocked to a young Julius Caesar, it always has been the young—and inebriated idealists—who make history. Sensing this history (and perhaps even more so the chance to be part of something ridiculous), I joined the Trump campaign as a volunteer, the vanguard of the douches who shook the world, to find out what made them tick and what the hell they were thinking.

Right away, I noticed that something about this presidential campaign was different than most: campaigns traditionally center on candidates with a lot of experience. Most serious presidential contenders previously have run for political office, served, and then run for reelection as congresspersons, senators, or governors. For the good or bad, they've spent years in Washington and state capitals, acquiring experience, donors, and seasoned campaign managers who expertly analyze "big data" and can easily name, off the top of their heads, a deputy ward leader in northeast Arkansas. Their campaigns are well-oiled machines, seasoned and honed over the course of decades and built upon the legacy of a democratic republic more than two centuries in the making.

The man behind Trump Steaks was not part of a traditional presidential campaign. Although its candidate was a purported billionaire, the Trump Campaign subsisted as a bare-bones, scrappy, and under-funded operation run out of a small office in Trump Tower virtually devoid of personnel. In fact, it hardly bothered to set up Trump headquarters in the respective capitals of most states, much less hire spokespeople. This candidate didn't expect to win and acted like it.

But no one bothered to tell his true believers—or Trump himself.

Blue Bell, Pennsylvania—near Valley Forge—is the kind of place where people gladly open their homes to complete strangers who knock on their doors. Well, just as long as they're white ... like eighty-five percent of Blue Bell's population.

As we stood in the center of the street, I realized that we three Trump volunteers would make the ultimate misfit softball team.

"I can't do this in the heat. I got asthma," complained the hunched-over Trump volunteer who carried a flip phone and use to work for Lockheed Martin. "I'm too old." I didn't have the heart to inform him that his preferred candidate pledged to repeal the Affordable Care Act—the Obama-era health program that, though a far cry from the national health plans common throughout the world—might partially subsidize his inhalers.

After the morning training session, which was held in a nearby bank office, our crew canvassed an all-American neighborhood adorned with pristine lawns and American flags. Like Jehovah's Witnesses, we knocked on doors and spread the political words of the conservative Republican Messiah, Donald J. Trump.

"People are afraid sometimes, going out and talking to voters as a Republican," shared our leader Brendon, a lanky guy with hyper-energy and a laugh that sounded like a disruptive lawnmower. As a local Republican Party staff member, he was what passed for a professional. "They feel like there is this massive elephant on their chest, and people whisper as they walk down the street. I've done about ten thousand doors. It doesn't happen. Trust me—it's not an issue."

Maybe so, but the previous time he canvassed for Trump, Brendon had the police called on him by a homeowner who thought that his gangly figure looked "dangerous." Unfazed and still a true Trump trooper, Brendon, alone the prior Saturday, knocked on three hundred fifty doors in the name of the orange one.

"Person-to-person—someone talking to them at their door—is better than a phone call. It's more effective to look at someone directly in the eyes," he said. "The challenge with Trump is reaching out to people who normally don't vote—so we have to find them first. And we'll find them door-to-door."

As we gathered around Brendon, he consulted the Trump app that we all had been ordered to download onto our phones. The app showed a map of the neighborhood, with a pin on each target home. The information it provided—names, addresses, and who each resident had voted for in the past (all compiled from the massive Republican Party database, petition drives, and purchased public information)—was creepy, almost stalker-esque. It, however, wasn't a novel approach: the Democratic Party started collecting mass voter data four years earlier.

"What makes a good voter?" asked the other new volunteer, a short Ukrainian guy. As a college business major, he had an unwholesome interest in pursuing politics.

"Our target voter, ultimately, it's white households," confirmed Brandon. Shock! I contemplated sneaking off to call CNN, thinking

Anderson Cooper might be interested in this inside scoop on the Trump campaign.

After each knocked door, we were supposed to make notes inside the app, indicating whether or not we should return there before the election.

"Jane McDonald. House twenty-one. She's female. She's voted in four of the past presidential elections. It says swing; she goes either way," Brendon read from the app.

"It's all about getting over the first step, knocking on the first door," he said, advising the newbies. "And the best part is—you get to talk to people who agree with you."

I concurred with a "Yup! Yup!" before adding Trump immigration rhetoric to make myself seem even more credible: "Get 'em out! Get 'em out! Build that wall! Build that wall."

We smiled, shared a laugh, and then huddled together—like an oddball band of crime fighters—to strike a plan.

"I don't think all of us should go up to the house," suggested the short Ukrainian kid as he stared at our mismatched group.

"Were you nervous the first time you went out?" I asked him.

"A little bit," he said. "You'll get used to it."

We stood in the street and watch Brendon and the hunched guy approach the targeted house. They knocked, and a man came to the door. "OH NO! NO! NOT THE REPUBLICANS!" the man loudly proclaimed before slamming the door in their faces.

"Is that how it usually goes?" I asked the Ukrainian kid.

"I don't say 'Republican.' I say, 'Political organization.' When you say, 'Republican,' people shut down," he whispered, as if it were privy information. "Or I say, 'I'm in a political organization asking questions.' It's vague—but you get the answers you want to get."

Even low-level Trump campaign workers were required to be disingenuous with the general public.

In the aftermath of defeat, Brandon confessed, "That was a quick 'no.' The Trump name is a turnoff."

As a result, Brendon advised using a smoke-and-mirrors strategy by first saying that we were volunteers for the local Republican candidate. Then, once we had their ears, he suggested working our way to admitting that we were from the Trump campaign.

"Other people say, 'I'm doing a survey of local people,'" he added. "Which is also true but a bit misleading."

If no one was home, we were supposed to leave the Trump pamphlet, which might be misconstrued by minorities as hate literature, on their door handle.

"What if someone is on the fence, and they don't think some of the things Trump says are racist and not politically correct?" I asked, emphasizing the last two words in a sarcastic voice while waving my hands in the air.

"Make it personal," Brendon suggested. "Say, 'I was really concerned because I heard Trump say this. But then I went on the Internet and saw the statement was on Twitter—so obviously, it didn't sound the most coherent.'"

After numerous rejections, the other two Trump volunteers bailed, leaving just the shock troops of the Trump Revolution: Brendon and me. At the previous house, once we mentioned Trump's name, the woman shut her front door and then rapidly closed her garage door. It was as if I had a big "Kick Me" sign tattooed on my forehead—or just a picture of Trump. These people didn't seem to enjoy having their lives interrupted by the word of Trump.

"What's the worst reaction you've ever received?" I asked Brendon as we walked to the next target.

"Usually people—who are so upset that you even dared to talk to them—they're not actually angry at you," he said. "They are upset that someone would actually talk to them about Trump."

Still, with all this rejection, what was Brendon's core motivation?

"I'm one of those people—if you give me two seconds—I'll care passionately about that issue. I'm a little bit unusual in that sense. I'm very pro-life," Brendon said. "I'm also really big on education because my mother is a teacher. It's not every day you get a Republican who is vested in education."

According to the app, the three occupants of the next house were all Republicans, but only one had voted in the last four general elections. Before Brendon knocked on the front door, he said a quick prayer, trying to get into the zone. Yes, it was a little weird.

Then, a dog started barking, and a middle-aged woman swung open the front door. Who the hell were these people that in 2016 blindly swung open their front doors to two grown, strange men?

"What issues do you care about in the upcoming election?" Brendon blurted.

"Pro-life. Military. The Army. Economy," the woman responded like a monotone conservative robot.

"How do you feel about Donald Trump?" asked Brendon.

"For him!" she replied. Victory!

We handed her a Trump flyer. Brendon was ecstatic as we walked away.

"That's an example of how things could not have gone better," he said. "Make a note of that in your phone."

On the Trump app, under house number forty-one, I typed: "Don't go back here. She might be Muslim! Call immigration!"

So, I apparently passed the test and was now ready to show new volunteers the ropes. Brendon said he was going to filter them my way. "I could see really getting into the swing of this," I said, lying through my teeth.

Before leaving, Brendon summed up canvassing for Trump in a world where even Republicans frowned upon him: "Usually most party members would vote Republican, but they need to have extra attention focused on them to vote Trump. They need motivation. That's why we're doing this stuff now—because we need to continue this stuff until October to win."

He handed me the clipboard and a stack of Trump flyers to take with me the next time I canvassed. But sadly, there would be no next time. I took the Trump flyers and, for effect, mumbled to Brendon, "Lying, crooked Hillary." As he drove away, I counted the seconds until I threw all of them into the recycle bin. My sabotage may have failed to block the rise of Trump, but the environment was richer for it.

BUILD A WALL AND GET 'EM OUT

PART TWO

INTRODUCTION
TRUMP ISN'T BLUFFING

MANY REPUBLICANS, AND NOT a few Democrats, have argued since the election that Donald Trump isn't serious. Trump himself often says that he stakes out extreme positions as a bargaining/dealmaking posture—that he likes to start far away from where he's willing to end up because it puts his opponents off-balance and gets him closer to his desired posture when a deal is finally made.

Maybe this is true. With Donald Trump, there's only one thing you can be sure of: when his lips are moving (or his Twitter feed is churning), you can't reasonably assume that anything he says is true. But there's a major problem with sleeping well at night based on the assumption that things can't turn out that bad: they can, and have, in the past. The United States, after all, attempted to exterminate an entire people (Native Americans), was the first and only nation to use nuclear weapons against civilian targets (twice), and is the only country on earth with at-will employment that allows employers to fire workers for no reason whatsoever. And don't forget the concentration camps where we interred Japanese-Americans during World War II and shipped "enemy combatants" (Guantánamo). We do extreme stuff all the time.

Democrats—being what they are, spineless and sniveling—often bend over backwards to accommodate Republican extremism on everything from attempts at gun control to invading Iraq to trickle-down economics. These days, Democrats are even willing to discuss Donald Trump's idea of building a Great Wall of America along the border with Mexico.

So, when people say Trump's weird ideas can't possibly come true, think again. They can. He *is* the President of the United States.

Please believe me when I say this gives me no pleasure: Donald Trump isn't bluffing when he threatens to deport the estimated eleven million people living in the U.S. illegally.

Are you undocumented? Prepare to go underground.

Are your papers in good standing? Are you a good person? Prepare a hiding place in your home.

Dark days are ahead.

Do not take comfort in the fact that Trump flip-flops on all sorts of issues. Contrary to his initial, typically strident position on abortion, the master demagogue now says women needn't fear imprisonment if they terminate their pregnancy (unless he changes his mind again). Even that much-ballyhooed Great Wall may wind up as half a wall. He does this a lot.

But he'll always want those mass deportations.

Why are deportations different for Trump? Radical nativism, as defined by this promise to deport illegal immigrants (every single one of them), defined his campaign from the start. It's why he's where he is. It's why he won.

Reneging on deportations would be like Bernie Sanders asking Goldman Sachs for donations or Hillary Clinton changing her gender —it would betray the raison d'être of his campaign. He can't back down without losing most of his support.

The optics of the biggest forced population movement since those carried out by Hitler and Stalin would be awful. Police kicking down doors. Women and children being dragged off in the middle of the night. Neighbors, friends, colleagues, lovers, spouses—disappeared.

Countries of origin would be reluctant to absorb millions of new arrivals, all unemployed, many of whom came to the U.S. as children and thus have no memories of their "home" countries. So the Trump Administration would have to build concentration camps to house them.

Because the idea is so outlandish, so fundamentally un-American, it's too much to contemplate seriously, even for journalists. They're in denial. Still, it's entirely possible that he will carry out his plan.

Legally, there's nothing to it. Trump doesn't need an act of Congress. He doesn't even have to sign an executive order. All he'd have to do to set this outrage in motion is pick up the phone and tell the head of Immigrations and Customs Enforcement to do his or her job: enforce the law. It's surprising that he didn't delegate that responsibility to his former chief of staff, retired general and amateur Civil War revisionist historian John Kelly, who ordered ICE to portray immigrants as criminals to justify raids

But camps cost money. So do more border agents. No problem. President Trump can shift his budget priorities in favor of ICE. He's already said he would triple ICE's enforcement division from five thousand to fifteen thousand officers. The FBI would have to pitch in.

Backlogs in the nation's fifty-seven existing immigration courts run as long as two years. The system would have to be expanded.

Speaking of which, I look to Trump's authoritarian impulse to turn initially to the federal budget. I suspect Trump will take advantage of the hysteria following a relatively serious terrorist attack attributed to a foreign national, especially one who turns out to have entered the country illegally. I imagine him making a pitch that goes like this:

I won because the American people wanted my business acumen in charge of government. Congress has totally messed up the budget process with their budget stand-offs. Sad. Let me take care of the budget, and I promise you an end to this crap. Take your kids to a national park, and I guarantee it won't be closed due to some government shutdown. Believe me.

Compliant media + perceived mandate + popular exhaustion = Trump gets his way.

Sad but true: subtracting eleven million people from the population, and thus two to four million from the workforce, could put money into the pockets of everybody else. Fewer workers, in theory, means labor has more clout. Wages could go up. Meanwhile, deportations would empty housing stock. Rents might decline. In the short term, anyway, Trumpism could stimulate the economy. That would be popular.

Establishmentarians can't imagine that Trump would actually go through with mass deportations, much less how he would carry them out. "I can't even begin to picture how we would deport eleven million people in a few years when we don't have a police state, where the police can't break down your door at will and take you away without a warrant," said Michael Chertoff, head of the Department of Homeland Security under George W. Bush.

You don't need imagination to game this out. You need history.

Right-wingers will call the cops to report their undocumented neighbors. As in Nazi-occupied Europe, anyone with a grudge against someone without a valid I-9 form will drop a dime to Trump's jackbooted thugs. Checkpoints will spring up on roads, at bus stops, in train stations. Mass surveillance by the NSA ensures that the feds know where illegals live. It won't be hard to find judges to issue warrants based on those reports.

For Trump, deportations are a political necessity he can easily execute. For his critics, they won't occur because they would run against our societal values. "Unless you suspend the Constitution and instruct the police to behave as if we live in North Korea," Chertoff said, "it ain't happening."

More than most people, Chertoff ought to know better. After all, he served under a radical right-wing president who convinced us to go along with perpetual war, concentration camps, legalized torture, invading foreign countries for fun, killer drone planes, and a new cabinet-level bureaucracy whose mission—and very name, Homeland Security—evokes Nazi Germany.

It doesn't take much to convince Americans to accept the unacceptable. We do it all the time.

–TED RALL

They may not be Nazis, but join **HARMON** as he infiltrates some folks who would prefer an all-white America ...

CHAPTER 4

ISLAMOPHOBES LOVE COOKIES

O N THE DAY OF the San Bernardino mass shooting, roughly forty-five people gathered clear across the country on Long Island, New York to discuss what they believed to be the problem with Muslims.

"What is being taught in the mosques is pure, pure, pure anti-American disgrace," seethed an angry man to a conference room full of red-faced Islamophobes in that redneck bastion of the Deep South known as Suffolk County: home of the Hamptons, which has a well-documented conservative streak and was a hotbed of Trump America during the 2016 presidential campaign.

A rumbling erupted through the crowd, followed by nods of agreement. While the volume of the rage was startling, the fact that some folks might not be partial to brown people was not. Soon, the room devolved into an AA-like support group, but instead of (or perhaps in addition to) a predisposition to the over-consumption of gin, the attendees shared something different in common: the fear that Muslims are about to take over America.

"We need to have a large undercover group going into mosques and film what's going on," added an older woman, whose voice resonated with an abrasive Long Island inflection, as others suggested how to expose local mosques for what they really are and what they're hiding from the public. "And you know what ... if they don't want to denounce Sharia Law, THE PLACE WILL BE CLOSED!"

Now that our country is being governed by the man who led the birther movement, claiming that his predecessor was a secret Muslim, a groundswell of racism against that faith has continued to grow.

I had infiltrated a meeting of ACT for America, an organization listed by the Southern Poverty Law Center as hate group "because it pushes wild anti-Muslim conspiracy theories, denigrates American Muslims, and deliberately conflates mainstream and radical Islam."

Founded in 2007 by Lebanese-born Brigitte Gabriel, whose birth name was Hanan Qahwaji, ACT for America claims to disavow racism, even though its loopy leader, a self-hating and self-professed "national security expert" on Fox News, gained mainstream notoriety by bashing Muslims. She has attempted to meld all Muslims with the actions of violent extremists: "Islamic terrorists ... are really just very devout followers of Muhammad. They are following his example and doing exactly what the Koran teaches and their mullahs exhort them to do."

ACT for America, which claims to be "the nation's largest nonprofit, non-partisan, grassroots national security organization with 750,000 members," doesn't blame extremism on "radical" Islam—but on Islam itself. The group's rhetoric generates fear by claiming that all Muslims, not just fringe extremists like members of ISIS and Al-Qaeda, seek to replace the Constitution with Islamic Sharia Law—the basic doctrine of the Qur'an—which is a personal, moral code for U.S. Muslims and not a specific political agenda.

No one needs to stress the horrors and sadness of a mass shooting (or any shooting for that matter), but ACT for America—a right-wing organization that draws from the NRA crowd—doesn't consider guns or gun legislation worthy of discussion. For them, the issue is religion (specifically Islam), despite the fact that the majority of mass shootings in the United States are committed by young, white American males who are often fanatical about Jesus.

The thought process of a typical Islamophobe goes something like this: "White people aren't as scary or crazy as Muslims, who look different and speak some gibberish language. And since we don't understand them or their culture, or their food, they, therefore, must be secretly plotting something devious in their non-white, non-Christian mosques."

To find out how people fan the flames of anti-Muslim rage, I headed to the nearest chapter meeting of ACT for America in conservative disguise (American flag T-shirt, American flag hat, American flag pin). I was sold by their tagline: "Our mission is to educate and effect change; people need to wake up."

Who could argue with such noble intent? It was time to wake up!

From ISIS-occupied Brooklyn—or were those radical Islamist terrorist-looking guys just Williamsburg hipsters?—I drove an hour and a half east to the seemingly innocuous bedroom community of Hauppauge on Long Island. Held at the Matrix Corporate Park, this meeting wasn't some top-secret klavern thing: I bought a ticket for twenty dollars on Eventbrite. If all that I had read about Act for America was true, then this gathering stood to offer me a window into the mainstream face of racism. The theme of the evening's program: "Who is the enemy and what is the enemy's 'Threat Doctrine?'" It may have been phrased in the form of a question, but everyone there knew who "the enemy" was—and most of them had made up their minds about how to stop them.

The conference room displayed a banner, front and center, that read: *Alert Long Island*. I took a seat amongst the group, directly behind a man in a camouflage Oath Keepers hat and next to another guy wearing a pro-gun T-shirt that broadcast: *Come & Get Them!*

Needless to say, the majority of the room—filled with old and white Tea Party types—would probably have backed up Trump's debunked claim of seeing "thousands and thousands" of Muslims cheering from New Jersey as the Twin Towers fell on September 11, 2001.

"In 2006, we began a study called Mapping Sharia," said the speaker, David Yerushalmi, who co-authored the project to back up his conspiracy theory that mosques are incubators of hate and urge their followers to overthrow the government. "Eighty percent of U.S. mosques are strictly Sharia inherent."

He calmly stressed that Muslims who pray at mosques are following the same violent "Death to America" dogma as an Al-Qaeda terrorist. "The core doctrine is still orthodox Sharia," he said. "It still utilizes the key methodology to achieve the end—or jihad."

I schlepped all the way to Outer Whitelandia for this race-bashing meeting, but Yerushalmi was being Skyped in from San Diego. This minor fact hadn't been mentioned on Eventbrite. I dished out an Andrew Jackson with the expectation that this Muslim racism was going to be live and in person, face-to-face, not projected on a screen via video chat. What a ripoff! Despite the ruse, Yerushalmi's message rang clear to the Alert Long Island members, who actively took notes and nodded their heads at key, hateful points. Who knew bigotry required so much studying? Was there going to be a test?

Yerushalmi is also on the Southern Poverty Law Center's watch list. As the attorney of choice for alt-right types, his credits include defending notable Qur'an-burning pastor Terry Jones. Yerushalmi once stated that "the mythical 'moderate' Muslim who embrace[s] traditional Islam but want[s] a peaceful coexistence with the West— is effectively non-existent" and that "most of the fundamental differences between the races are genetic."

He spoke in a low-key academic tone, claiming that if a Muslim attends an American mosque, then he is not only learning a violent doctrine but is also susceptible to being recruited by ISIS ... because that's what Muslims do!

"The problem we face is global, and it's local. The ability of Islamic terrorist groups to recruit will continue. Until there is some kind of internal reformation in Islam—to create an institutional counter to Sharia," he said, describing a quandary, "they will always be able to reach into any Muslim community—anywhere in the world—and recruit."

Did he not know that the primary goal of Al-Qaeda was to restore the caliphate in order to provide spiritual and legal guidance to Islam's disparate millions?

Yerushalmi's next fearful call to action directly hit home to the tune of Trump rally proportions: "By opening the gates to Muslim immigration, it's quite simple. The more Muslims that immigrate to the West, the greater the likelihood that they will come ready to be recruited. Or they come already recruited ... as a sleeper cell."

ACT for America attendees let out an audible moan and gave each other a "not in our backyard" look.

This rhetoric has contributed to the rise in vandalism and violent threats made against North American mosques. For example, hours after the Paris attacks in November 2015, a mosque in St. Petersburg, Florida received a voicemail from a man who said he planned to shoot Muslims, including children, in the head.

"The real threat from Syrians is not that ISIS will slip in secret agents—it is that the Syrian immigrants, when they come here, where are they going to go? To those mosques," Yerushalmi warned, regarding the displaced war refugees—largely women and children—who are fleeing because they're afraid of ... ISIS.

"The reservoir of support is there. So recruitment is always going to be a resource for Islamic jihad—as long as it exists as it does today," he continued.

Yerushalmi raised the fear factor by generalizing the beliefs of the world's one billion five hundred thousand Muslims and promoting the notion that mosques are nothing but "Death to America" factories.

"The threat is real! They don't want peace and prosperity," he concluded with more broad strokes. "They want to live by Sharia. Sharia is not a peaceful, feel-good Islam."

Unwittingly, I once again looked at the T-shirt on the guy in front of me and whispered it to myself: "Come & Get Them!"

When it was time for questions, the doors of anger and paranoia flew open. "Shame, shame!" cried an older woman as she stood up to address the room. "If we know these mosques are radical—shame, shame on us!"

The moderator consoled her: "Well, we didn't know for sure until recently."

Clearly agitated, the lady continued: "If my Roman Catholic Church would be preaching death to Muslims, Jews, everyone else—I'm sure it would be closed down with a blink of an eye! So this is where we have to stop the growth of mosques!"

An older woman interrupted. "Do you know about the mosque in Melville? Does everyone know about the mosque in Melville?" she asked as her voice got louder and her body pivoted to open up the question to the rest of the group.

"Okay, so why is that mosque going up!?" questioned the first outraged old woman with disbelief.

"They're using our system—and this is the genius of it—to get religious freedom," explained the moderator. "They're working it better than we're working it."

As the momentum and anger in the room grew, the floodgates of Islamophobia opened wide, and conspiracy theories abounded. A Long Island housewife voiced concern over a local Islamic Center opening a dialogue with a public school in an attempt to educate the kids about their religion. "Do you have any suggestions on how to counter that—how to come up with a counter strategy?" she asked, barely containing her rage. "Is there any legalities we could exploit and such!?"

If this were another era, the threat of foreigners would be focused on other ethnic groups—the "unruly" Irish, the "shifty" Chinese, or the "tawny" Germans, who refused to be Americanized—instead of the adherents of Islam. ACT for America's rhetoric resembled that of a century ago, when immigrant Jews were seen as a direct threat to Western values.

"A religious minority is seen as a dangerous underclass destroying society from below with their alien values, as well as a hidden force secretly controlling the world from above, through their infiltration of centres of power," wrote Arun Kundnani in a 2015 *Al Jazeera* article, which drew parallels between the past treatment of Jews and ACT for America's angry Muslim discourse.

"They don't want peace and prosperity. They want to live by Sharia," chimed in an angry old man echoing Yerushalmi's exact words, as the use of "they" began to ring with the same intonation as the n-word.

"When they say 'peace,' what do they mean?" asked the woman who helped organize the event. To clarify matters, she offered to provide a Sharia translation guide to help break down secret Muslim code words.

"What 'peace' means to them—it's when they take over the world. That's peace," clarified the moderator to audible moans. "When they say 'protection of the innocent,' they mean ONLY Muslims. When you translate it from what they mean, it's like 'kill the infidels and we're taking over!'" she said to more moans.

The room ate up this hyperbole, despite the fact that the need for gun control was never mentioned, nor the fact that people on the TSA's no-fly list still have the "right" to buy firearms.

"The word 'taqiyya' is what really bothers me. It means you lie to get ahead—to get what you want," said an old guy who was now addressing the room. "This word, 'taqiyya'—Lie! Lie! Lie! So how can you believe anything they say? Because anything these people say is just the opposite."

The man continued: "I got a fantasy ever since I discovered some of the verses in the Koran. Drop leaflets from the sky in Arabic that say, 'There is no paradise,' or some kind of statement that's going to discredit the Koran. But in multitudes—all at one time—and cause chaos in the Muslim world. That's my fantasy."

We're all entitled to our fantasies.

A loud applause erupted from the room. It was beginning to feel as if the villagers were about to grab their rakes and torches, storm the streets, and go after Frankenstein's monster. I double-checked my disguise and looked for the nearest exit.

After the meeting, the room buzzed and adrenaline flowed amongst these like-minded citizens. An evening of singling out and stereotyping Muslims—and fueling anger towards the community—had everyone there pumped up and ready to kick Muslim ass.

As anti-Muslim rumblings continued to fill the room, I distanced myself from the mob and moved towards the cookie table. (Yes, Islamophobes love cookies.)

It was crazy, the different tiers of hate present—from academic voices and sheltered suburban housewives to lone wolves ready to take action.

"We'll do it!" exclaimed a woman in regards to organizing a rally against Syrian refugees. I was informed that she ran a splinter group called Conservative Society for Action. "That's something we could do. We need at least a week."

Her husband piped in: "Yes! Yes! Yes!"

"They get uppity," blurted the glossy-eyed and hardened old man standing next to me near the cookie table. "If they don't get put in their place, they get uppity."

I politely nodded, smiled, and then took a bite of a cookie baked by a bigot.

Mmmm, tasty.

"They have a history of what they do in these countries," he continued with conviction. "If you've seen what they do in France—they take control. Otherwise, they're very quiet—when there's just a few of them."

I uttered, "Uh-huh," and nodded my head.

"This will still be going on long after I'm gone," the old guy said with added intensity. "But maybe I can take a few of them out with me … maybe I can take a few of the out with me …"

As I chomped on another scrumptious cookie, a woman handed

me a flyer printed with bold red lettering that read: **TAKE YOUR COUNTRY BACK!** So much nationalistic subtext in so few words.

Now that I had my twenty dollars worth out of this meeting, it was time to go.

Back in my car, I turned on the radio and learned more shocking details about San Bernardino: the shooters were self-radicalized Muslim terrorists. Saddened by the state of humanity, I departed the Matrix Corporate Media Center and a group of anti-Muslim activists who were ready to take violent action against an entire faith of people.

CHAPTER 5

ANGRY VILLAGERS CHASING ALIENS

NATIVISM—FEAR OF FOREIGNERS coupled with the desire to prioritize native-born citizens over newcomers—was at the core of Donald Trump's campaign, beginning with his 2015 announcement that he was planning to run for president. Trump campaigned and won in large part on his promise to build a "big, beautiful" wall along America's border with Mexico.

Trump wasn't original. He glommed onto an old controversy familiar to residents of southern California, Texas, and the Southwest—a conundrum with which they have long had to grapple: leaving the border largely unpatrolled in order to fulfill the desire for cheap labor provided by Mexicans and other Latin Americans who crossed illegally. But the newcomers were often hardworking and willing to do so for low pay, which caused resentment among some Americans.

At the tip of the spear of the latter is the Minutemen—a paramilitary "militia" group that emerged from the gun-toting right to do what it believed the U.S. government wasn't willing to do: keep foreigners from crossing the southern border into the good ole U.S.A.

But the good ole U.S.A. is often described as "a land of immigrants." My grandparents came to the U.S. from the old country, escaping Nazis.

America said to them, "Come on in. You're welcome here."

Of course, my grandparents were lucky. The U.S. denied asylum to most Jews fleeing Hitler, including the passengers of the German ocean liner St. Louis, who were turned back to Europe, where more than a quarter died in Nazi death camps.

For a land of immigrants, the U.S. doesn't have a stellar track record when it comes to immigration. The Chinese Exclusion Act of 1882 banned Chinese workers from entering the country, and the Immigration Act of 1917 barred immigration from the Asia-Pacific Zone.

These horrors rang through my head as I gathered with infuriated American citizens who were ready for the U.S. government to do its job and fix the immigration "problem."

Standing in front of a flapping American flag and screaming into a microphone, a Minuteman from Southern California looked seriously angry. He was foaming at the mouth pissed off as he directed his attention to the press, or "fake news," evincing even more passionate disgust than the previous speakers had shown at the thought of illegal aliens entering their neighborhoods.

"It's the media that's the other half of the problem in this country for not covering the story THE WAY IT REALLY IS!!!!" he screamed, echoing a sentiment that later became standard go-to fare for Trump.

Sitting at long rows of picnic tables, the Minutemen—private vigilantes who have been patrolling the Mexican border to spot illegal aliens—started thunderously whistling and jeering. This barbecue marked the closing of the Minuteman Project's month-long patrol, so the crowd, which consisted of potbellied elderly white men and their scary wives, was going apeshit.

Infuriated that news outlets have painted the Minutemen as gun-toting, racist yahoos, the irate speaker pointed in the direction of the media—several well-groomed local reporters, various photographers, and, of course, Fox News—and screamed, "SO WHY DON'T YOU FOLKS PACK UP AND GO SOUTH OF THE BORDER WHERE YOU WANT TO BE CONTROLLED!"

The angry mob began throwing out taunts and heckles at the press.

"Traitors!"

"Sorry excuses for Americans!"

"Bye-bye media!"

It seemed as if someone were about to yell, "GET THEM!"

Before being faced with the prospect of going south of the border where I wanted to be controlled, I traveled to Tombstone, Arizona to infiltrate the men and women behind the Minuteman Project. Surprisingly, there were no Minutekids. Sure, I had heard the news descriptions of vigilantes hunting down illegal aliens like a white supremacist lynch mob in the Jim Crow South. But I also had heard others defending the Minutemen, claiming that they were just a bunch of harmless senior citizens who spent their twilight years sitting in lawn chairs along the southern border. To me, the whole thing sounded like a big, three-ring, anti-immigration circus. And when armed vigilantes are the ringmasters under the Mexican-border big top, I never miss the circus.

Dressed as a Minuteman—complete with aviator shades and matching Army-fatigue shirt, shorts, and hat—I arrived at the project's headquarters, only a few blocks from the historic O.K. Corral, for the morning orientation session on the twenty-eighth day of the their month-long Mexican border jamboree.

"I'm going to ask you a pertinent question: are you armed?" asked a large, intimidating man with a gun strapped across his chest. No need to ask him the same silly question.

I quickly took a visual inventory of my body before firmly answering: "No!"

In the yard behind the office, eighteen Minutemen—all with serious, okay grim, looks on their faces—were assembled, including a hardened grandmother and an unhappy woman, who was half of an unhappy couple. Most of the vigilantes were dressed like me and displayed nervous uneasiness, as if they were about to be shipped off to war and might not return.

Under the hot Arizona sun, I took a chair behind an old guy whose T-shirt read: **Retired—I Can Play With My Trains Anytime I Want**.

"This is not about skinheads. This is not about the KKK. We are here to observe and report," began the orientation from the irate man, who spoke as if he were reciting a legal disclaimer. I looked around to see if anyone was disappointed by this assertion.

Next, the Minuteman mission statement was laid out: "The Constitution says protect our borders from the threat of invasion. We have the right to freedom of assembly."

Mustachioed Tex, costumed in standard cowboy hat and boots, spoke up: "Is that a Minuteman rule or an ACLU rule that you can't return fire if fired upon?"

The intimidating man answered, "We want the operation to be clean."

Unsatisfied, Tex asked, "If I'm fired upon, isn't that imminent danger?"

The large man—whose green shirt was flapping in the wind, exposing his huge belly—provided vague encouragement to Tex: "I can't tell you what to do!"

Tex's inquiry then opened up a series of anti-immigration, dumb white guy questions.

"What's better: to have them see us and go around, or shine a light and scare them back to Mexico?" asked a Minuteman named Russ. "What's preferable?"

The answer: "Shine a light and let them know you're there."

In a slight panic, Russ followed up: "What if you shine a light on them, and then they come after you?" He was quickly cut off after segueing into a long rambling political diatribe.

Our orientation leader stressed one final rule: "No contact. Anyone has contact, they're gone."

Apparently, some Minutemen were kicked out of the project for giving water to illegal aliens who had traveled on foot for days through the hot desert. The large man, who didn't appear to have missed many meals, explained that this type of decent behavior would "jeopardize the whole program."

The orientation leader concluded with this insight: "I'm going to look everyone in the eye, and I'm going to ask two questions. Do you agree to stick with the rules and what we're about, which is about the Constitution and securing our borders?"

I hated to break the news (so I didn't), but that was really only one question. When it came my turn, the leader looked me directly in the eyes, and I responded by reading the phrase from the T-shirt of the man in front of me: "What part of illegal don't they understand?"

At the last, hot and dusty outpost before the border, I stood in triple-digit heat amongst a bunch of concerned citizens, including a burly guy whose T-shirt read: **Be There in a Minute ... Man!** Most in the group were lone men, who felt a call of duty and came out there on their own, from all parts of the country.

The line supervisor, who had a gray beard and incongruously wore a Fidel Castro hat, noted that the night shift—ten o'clock at night to six o'clock in the morning—was the busiest time to patrol but also the most unpopular. "You may get a bit lonely. You might have a few Mexicans to keep you company. The coyotes sit on the hills watching us, where we don't have people," he said, referring to the guides who charge money—anywhere from three hundred to eleven hundred dollars on this part of the border—to lead immigrants from Mexico into the United States. "Since we've come out here, we heard the price has doubled."

Next, we were led to a grown man named "Papa Bear," who was clad in tinted shades and prominently wore a gun on his belt and radio wires and military insignias on his vest. Papa Bear slightly resembled Robert Duvall's character, Colonel Kilgore, in *Apocalypse Now*. But instead of arriving in a Huey, this sixty-four-year-old former member of the Army's 82nd Airborne Division showed up driving a tiny Mazda Miata.

With clipboard in hand, Papa Bear commenced his briefing.

I wanted for him say, "I love the smell of napalm in the morning." Instead, he asked, "Anyone armed?"

Most hands went up.

"Be cool. If you have side arms, don't touch it unless you are certain that you're about to be killed," Papa Bear said.

Pointing to a kindly old woman, he proclaimed, "Phoebe assisted in a capture after midnight. Thirteen were captured."

Phoebe smiled proudly.

"We spotted a few coming under the wire. We called the Border Patrol. It was great for us to know that actually we got to assist in a tactical maneuver, as opposed to hearing about how someone else did it," Papa Bear added. "Made my day. All of us were calm, cool, collected during the operation. But when it was over, you had that prize, that package of thirteen captured. The adrenaline was flowing."

A young couple from San Diego, whose adrenaline decidedly was not flowing, already seemed bored. "There's sure a lot of standing around," one of them said with a sigh, disappointed that they were not experiencing the same kind of "action" as Phoebe.

Papa Bear expressed concern about the dope smugglers, the human flesh smugglers, and, of course, the terrorists. "They found copies of the

Koran and Arabic ID cards in the cleanup area," he stated, generating xenophobic paranoia. Not only was he implying that radical Islamist terrorists were sneaking into our country via the Mexican border but that they were so absent-minded and blasphemous that they kept losing copies of their holy book.

An old guy in a gray T-shirt confessed to Papa Bear, "I was in town today, and I almost wanted to catch some of the Mexicans who are already over here!"

After the briefing, eight of us in seven vehicles followed a convoy of large trucks down a dusty dirt road headed to the Naco Line (so named for the Arizona border town).

"Please move the radio away from your mouth when you talk into it," the Naco leader advised an old lady.

The Naco Line, basically a barbed-wire fence along the border, was torn open at numerous spots, thus providing approximately enough space for a blindfolded toddler to crawl through.

"Historically, this is one of the highest traffic areas," said the line supervisor, pointing to a large span of desert and mountains in the distance.

As the wind embedded dust between my teeth, I inquired about the relationship between the Minutemen and Border Patrol.

"Super-friendly. Last night they let me look through their night scopes," the supervisor said with a giddy smile.

Before sending us off on our own, he offered this last bit of advice: "When you leave here, make sure you don't back over any migrants, 'cause they'll be right behind you."

It was finally time to spot illegal aliens.

"It's actually been kind of boring, because nobody has tried to cross since we've been here," said a Texas trucker who had his rig parked in front of his tent. "But I like camping, so this suits me."

This part felt like an illegal-immigration-spotting summer camp.

"The big problem I have with it—they're dragging the U.S. down," shared a guy in an NRA hat. He, too, mentioned that several Minutemen had found copies of the Qur'an and Arabic flight schedules.

While driving down the dusty border road, I waved at the Minutemen, who joyfully waved back. I parked next to a van that displayed in the rear window two cardboard, hand-scrawled signs, which read: **Badges. We don't need no stinking badges!** and **WE HAVE THE CONSTITUTION.**

"A boring day is a good day," remarked Ken, an ex-cop from Arkansas, who—with his long white hair and thick mustache—looked like an old hippie. Recently, he reported movement at an abandoned ranch nicknamed the Naco Hilton and was therefore responsible for stopping forty pounds of not-pot—what Border Patrol playfully calls cocaine—from coming across the border.

"When the Border Patrol first heard we were coming, they said, 'That's great. All we need is a bunch of hillbillies out there, drinking, waving guns,'" he remarked with self-deprecating humor. "But after the third day, they knew that was not what it was."

A male nurse from Utah—who despite his wife's disapproval came out to the border anyway—excitedly asked, "Do you want to see some garbage left by people who have come by?"

I enthusiastically answered, "Sure!" hoping that the trash pile would contain a copy of the Qur'an and an Arabic flight schedule. Instead, there was a plastic bag weighted down by a rock and one tiny shoe. We stared at it for several seconds. All right then! It was a plastic bag and a tiny shoe, neither of which had Arabic writing.

Thus far, only one major incident had occurred, according to the Utah nurse: "There was this guy. He called himself "The Jokester." He made a T-shirt that said: *I Caught an Illegal Alien at the Border & All I Got Was This Lousy T-Shirt*. The Jokester then found an illegal alien, made him put on the T-shirt, and took photos."

The Minutemen attempt at humor was, thus far, the highlight of the night shift, which was not unlike sitting in one's car, listening to right-wing talk radio, and being extremely bored. After a while, though, I started to get a little jittery from drinking loads of coffee and started seeing things in the dark void that is the border. Good thing I wasn't armed!

Finally, we had some action. A message came over the walkie-talkie: "I'm going to move my car. Don't panic if you see some lights."

With a chuckle, another Minuteman replied, "I'll try not to get too trigger-happy."

I pushed the talk button on my walkie-talkie and said in a panic, "I'M FREAKIN' OUT MAN! I'M REALLY FREAKIN' OUT HERE," which was kind of, sort of true.

There was silence from the other end. Then, finally, "Do you need some security backup?"

While fiddling with my car radio, I accidentally flashed my car's lights. "There's someone flashing their lights towards the border," an urgent-sounding man, going by the name "Wisconsin," blurted over the radio. Wisconsin thought it was some sort of illegal-alien-rendezvous-meet-up signal.

"Do you want backup?" answered base headquarters.

"CALL IN THE AIRSTRIKE! CALL IN THE AIRSTRIKE!" I screamed into my walkie-talkie.

Over the radio, someone else said, "I just saw some lights. I'm going to go investigate!"

Maybe we had actually spotted our first illegal alien of the evening?! The radio transmitted again: "This is Gooseberry Down, just south of you. I didn't see no lights, but I'm walking towards ya."

A few moments later, big chuckles concerning the light emanated from the radio: "I just moved my position from in the trees, and it turned out to be the moon."

A couple of seconds later, to add drama to the affair, I screamed, "MAN DOWN! MAN DOWN!" Sadly, the Minutemen were sharp cookies. No one was buying it.

The Minuteman Project's closing barbecue was a big clappity-clap fest, with a lot of patriotic American flag-waving and God-blessing

America. The turnout was good. The parking lot was full of big trucks covered in bumper stickers that made political statements, such as: *CNN Lies*.

The closing started with the Pledge of Allegiance. Then, a pastor gave a valediction in the name of Jesus—because, as we all know, the one thing that Jesus would really, really want is secure borders.

That spectacle was followed by a series of really patriotic and inspiring speeches and the Minutemen patting each other on the backs for being such brave American heroes. An inspired Minuteman, adorned in a jean vest with red sleeves popping out, came to the microphone and said, "Those who do not respect our borders shall be repelled by force if it is necessary! I have stood shoulder to shoulder with heroes of America—you are it!"

I think he was expecting a *Dead Poets Society*-style slow, building round of thunderous applause and people eventually standing on the lunch tables. Sadly, it didn't happen. Instead, the guy woodenly added, "People ask, 'Aren't you afraid of getting killed?' I tell them, 'Fear is for those who sit home and watch reality television. THE MINUTEMEN HAVE NO FEAR!'"

If the American flag could smile, it would have been grinning from ear to ear.

Finally, we arrived at the part where things became really ugly: the patriotic, adrenaline-pumping crowd turned on the media.

Adorned in an ill-fitting baseball cap, the oldest man there—this guy was so old that he looked as if he were about to fall over—was a religious broadcaster who had been "battling the leftists" since 1961. He grabbed the microphone, sternly raised his voice, and pointed out the other true enemy of America: the liberal fake news. "I went into religious broadcasting so I could TELL THEM WHAT I THINK OF THEM!" he yelled, almost to the point where I thought he might wind up clutching his heart and toppling over.

"Yah!"

"The left-wing media is the biggest problem we got in America!" he continued.

"Woo! Yah!"

Just then, a large man—with a Bowie knife strapped to his hip—started looking over my shoulder as I jotted down notes. He purposely eyeballed me in an intentional attempt of intimidation. I felt his anger and fear.

So, there was really only one thing left for me, as an intrepid reporter, to do: pack up my gear and head south of the border, where I wanted "to be controlled!"

CHAPTER 6

KKK RESTAURANTS MAKE GREAT PIES

WHILE TRAVELING ALONG THE backroads of Trump America, it's not uncommon to see local businesses with signs stating: *American Owned and Operated.* If you read between the lines, these establishments are basically winking and saying, "Don't worry, fellow white person. You won't be doing business with stinky immigrants or colored folk; you will be hanging out with people who probably voted for Donald Trump."

In an earlier era, the racism of roadside America wasn't as subtle. The romanticized Route 66 of Jim Crow America gave rise to a sea of segregated businesses that now point an arrow to the unabashed rise of Trump-empowered white nationalism. Constructed in 1926 as a twenty-four hundred mile roadway that connected Chicago with Los Angeles, the "Road of Dreams"—as Route 66 was soon nicknamed—signified the freedom of the open road. But only if you were white.

During the 1930s, forty-four of the eighty-nine counties along Route 66 were "Sundown Towns," all-white communities that banned

African Americans from entering city limits after dark. Cities along the route placed racist messages on tourist postcards. In Edmond, Oklahoma postcards proudly boasted: *"A Good Place to Live." 6,000 Live Citizens. No Negroes.* It doesn't take answering the riddle of the Sphinx to know who their target demographic was (and was not).

To spell out exactly who was not welcome on the premises, some Route 66 establishments intentionally used the letters KKK in their business names. Kozy Kottage Kamp and Klean Kountry Kottages, blazoned with bold KKK capital letters that carried little innuendo, catered to whites only—since their branding was obvious code for the Ku Klux Klan. In plain view of the public, these establishments wanted to trumpet subtly (or not so subtly) the fact that they were associated with the KKK—and perhaps had plenty of meeting space in the backroom, including a laundry to clean sheets. If white wasn't your color, it was wise to steer clear.

The majority of these establishments are now closed. Yet several Triple K restaurants still exist as remnants of a bygone era of brazen intolerance, exclusion, Confederate statue praise, and good ol' plain white supremacy. In isolated towns in the South, there's Kathy's Kountry Kitchen, Koffee Kup Kafe, and Kathy's Kountry Korner.

"Frankly, these people live in a very different world. They've not dealt with any cultural diversity," said Nelson Linder, President of the Austin, Texas branch of the NAACP. "So, yes. Those symbols are very outdated, obviously, and not appropriate. I understand why they exist, and there is no pressure there to take them down—and there is no economic consequence."

It's hard to determine whether these eateries are making a racist statement or simply going for a cutesy misspelled name, like Toys R Us. Maybe we're reading too much into it—like that Illuminati pyramid on the back of money.

As Linder suggested, one way to find out is to look at the history and demographics of the town. For example, a café situated on Main Street in Noel, Missouri—a small and remote Ozark town of two thousand people located not too far from Harrison, Arkansas (the headquarters of the KKK)—originally opened in the 1970s. Throughout the years it has had a few different owners. Recently, the café reverted to its original name: Kathy's Kountry Kitchen.

"Kathy's has the best breakfast in town, hands down," a woman who works at the Noel City Hall excitedly informed me. She said their specialty is the chicken fried steak. I certainly didn't see blackened catfish on the menu.

Vivian Brooks, owner of Kathy's, said that she wanted to keep the original name of the restaurant in order to preserve history. When asked in an interview if the building was a former Ku Klux Klan meeting place, Brooks said that she had no idea whether that was true or not. But she did admit that she has been called racist for restoring the original name of the café, which she re-christened Kathy's Kountry Kitchen in 2006.

"I'm not going to change history," said Brooks, invoking the same *historic* argument used by those who support the Confederate Flag. "I'm just proud of my town."

On the post-1955 side of the racial divide, Linder and the NAACP feel that there's an appropriate place for these historic symbols of America's shameful past: "Museums. If you want to have a museum of these artifacts, that's okay—but not in public and private institutions. People have to be sensitive on what they're doing and they're not."

While Kathy's Kountry Kitchen may contain an ambiguous connection to the Klan, the eatery's servers wear T-shirts emblazoned with less subtle racist rhetoric: ***I got caught eating at the KKK***.

In Noel, a town just two miles square, an influx of refugees has changed the cultural landscape. During the late 2000s, Somali refugees began moving into Noel to work at the nearby Tyson food slaughterhouse. Some locals welcomed these new transplants and victims of war by slashing their tires. In recent years, local Somalis have said that they are not welcome at Kathy's Kountry Kitchen.

"It's inappropriate, but it's also a cultural thing based on a certain kind of arrogance," said Linder. "The fact that they are not under any kind of scrutiny, they are way out of the norm of society."

According to Linder, it could be dangerous in these isolated towns to express opposition to these so-called historic symbols: "They've been allowed to do that based on where they are."

Hico, Texas has a reputation of being the second most racist place in the state—only behind Vidor. The locale has an infamous history as a Sundown Town, including a local bank that once displayed a mural depicting a lynching scene. Not surprisingly, ninety percent of its fifteen hundred residents are white.

Numerous public cross burnings have taken place in Hico, which is located in Hamilton County, long thought to be the Texas seat of the KKK. One such event in 1992 attracted roughly three hundred attendees, who, after a long night of burning crosses, got pretty hungry and worked up a hankering for some ... delicious pies. Why not dine at a restaurant that bares their same initials: KKK?

Welcome to the Koffee Kup Kafe, a local favorite frequented by residents who hope that Trump will **Make America Great Again**—like it was in 1862 before the Emancipation Proclamation. Owned by a family that has lived in the area for generations, the restaurant was established in 1968—the same year Martin Luther King was assassinated—and features a large backroom, which has been reported to be a meeting place for Klansmen. A Twitter search tells the story:

> *broke down in Hico texas. so they went to a coffee shop called the Koffee Kup Kafe which is a kkk meet up place*

> *There is a Klan hangout spot 30 minutes from where I went to high school called the Koffee Kup Kafe lived in Hico Texas until 2007 or so the main cafe in town was still called the Koffee Kup Kafe. Post racial society is a myth.*

"The best thing is their pies," said Amanda Rekenwith, a Seattle transplant who admittedly dines at the Koffee Kup and is, therefore, using an obvious pseudonym. "People drive from miles around for the pies."

Technically, the Koffee Kup Kafe rebranded its name to the Koffee Kup Family Restaurant. "It is common knowledge that the original name was a nod to the KKK," Rekenwith confirmed. But there's still something very strange about the sign outside the diner: the icon of a man sitting at a table combined with his chair resembles the letter "K."

"Look at the sign, and it's easy to see that the third 'K' is still there," Rekenwith said. "Look at the odd posture of the cowboy sitting at the table in their logo. It's an inside joke."

Inside the Koffee Kup, the only overtly racist symbols are the salt and pepper shakers—portraying stereotypical depictions of African Americans—which hang on the wall. "Picture a minstrel show black man and Aunt Jemima, with exaggerated features," Rekenwith said.

During her numerous visits to the Koffee Kup Kafe, Rekenwith has always been greeted with kindness. "I am a white woman. So we were quite welcome," she said. "I never saw any customers who were people of color there. I did hear the use of racial slurs by locals while

I was there, usually in the context of what they considered a joke—or simply being descriptive."

Sure, Rekenwith once overheard a customer comment to a friend, "Don't be a nigger and stick me with the tab, Ronnie!" And another who referred to a Latino employee as a "beaner" and a "wetback." But did we mention those pies are amazing?

"These places are from a bygone era. But that's not an excuse," said Linder. "Because, in America today, we have to show a certain amount of respect for all people. It's part of our Constitution. And as long as those symbols remain, it's going to imply also that they accept a certain type of discrimination."

But according to Rekenwith, these racist symbols don't seem to matter to the Koffee Kup's customers. "Regardless of their history, the restaurant is always packed—any day of the week and any time from open to close," she said. "On the positive side, I just can't say enough about the pies."

Yes. Think of the pies. Think of the chicken fried steak. Think of the white, white mashed potatoes—as white as their preferred clientele —while you salivate over the pies at the KKK.

CHAPTER 7

MUSLIM? NO GUNS FOR YOU!

PRESIDENT OBAMA ONCE REMARKED that some Americans cling to their religion and their guns, but that order might be mistaken. For Second Amendment purists who listen to Rush Limbaugh, watch Fox News, and nervously await the jackbooted thugs of the federal *gubament* to come charging through their doors in order to confiscate their firearms, gun culture is a real thing. These voters form the hardcore GOP/Trump base and the target demographic of Crocket Keller's business model.

In his radio ad, which aired in Mason, Texas in spring 2017, Keller sounded like a kindly small town sheriff in an old, Western movie while promoting a concealed-carry course offered at his gun range in this predominantly white town of about two thousand people.

"It's family friendly," he said, noting that "all" are welcome. However, Keller, who, much like Trump, does not believe in political correctness, clarified: "If you are a non-Christian Arab or Muslim, I will not teach you the class."

As George Orwell observed, some people are more part of "all" than others.

At first, Keller's belief—that Islam is fundamentally un-American—seemed counter to the core American principle of freedom of religion, but he devised a foolproof method to ensure that Muslims don't attend his course. "We will offer a prayer for our country and a safe class, along with reciting the Pledge of Allegiance," he explained. "If you don't love and respect the United States of America, you're in the wrong place!"

The gun shop owner's conception of American-ness as something exclusively white (and Christian) aligns with a long, shameful American narrative of things Americans have done to those who are different? From the internment of Japanese-Americans during the Second World War to the "Whites Only" lunch counters of the Jim Crow South, exclusion has always been a part of how some Americans define themselves.

Now, another form of exclusion is thriving in some American businesses: no Muslim zones. Much like *No Irish Need Apply* signs of the 19th century, actual business establishments, including an ice cream store in rural Minnesota, are unabashedly trumpeting roadside signs that read: **Muslims Get Out**. However, these Muslim bans are found most frequently in ... gun stores.

According to Veronica Laizure, Civil Rights Director of the Oklahoma Chapter of the Council on American-Islamic Relations (CAIR), there is "sort of a disturbing trend of businesses declaring themselves to be a Muslim-free zone—or declaring that they are going to decline services to people who are Muslim."

Anti-Muslim bias is on the rise throughout American society. "Normalizing discrimination against American Muslims results in concrete acts of discrimination," Laizure added. "We have seen increases in discrimination both here and nationally as a trend since the last presidential campaign."

Anti-Muslim gun stores defend their actions by using this logic: "You wouldn't teach a 9/11 hijacker how to fly." No, of course you wouldn't. But would you inform a Muslim pilot in the U.S. Air Force how to fly a bomber over an ISIS controlled region?

Despite the fact that on American soil you're about six times more likely to be killed by lightning than by a foreign-born terrorist, gun store owners typically cite security concerns as the main reason for banning Muslims. Take, for example, Jan Morgan, owner of the Gun Cave in Hot Springs, Arkansas, who wrote on her website that she bans Muslims from her store for her own safety:

> *The Koran (which I have read and studied thoroughly) and (which muslims [sic] align themselves with), contains 109 verses commanding hate, murder and terror against all human beings who refuse to submit or convert to Islam.*

She, however, did not mention the abundance of passages in the Qur'an that call for peace or the stories of violence in the Bible and other religious texts.

So, how do store owners, such as Morgan, figure out which customers are Muslim? Unsurprisingly, by engaging in racial stereotyping.

For example, in 2015, a father and son of South Asian descent entered the Gun Cave only to be told by Morgan that it was a Muslim-free shooting range—and that if they were Muslim, then they should leave. When the father informed Morgan that they weren't Muslims, she reportedly kicked them out anyway and threatened to call the police, saying, "I don't think you guys should be here!"

The First Amendment allows businesses to post a *No Muslims* sign in their windows, but they cross the line legally if (and when) they act upon it by denying services based on one's ethnicity.

Thus far, most store owners who have refused to serve Muslims—or anyone they believe to be Muslim—haven't faced legal consequences. But thanks to Laizure, Muslim free zones are facing a test in court. She is one of the attorneys working on a federal lawsuit against Save Yourself Survival and Tactical Gun Range, a gun store in Oktaha, Oklahoma that in July 2015 posted a sign declaring itself a *Muslim-Free Establishment*.

Three months later, Raja'ee Fatihah, a Muslim-American U.S. Army reservist, visited the range with plans to use the facility. At first, the staff was friendly to Fatihah. But after he identified himself as Muslim, the gun store owners grabbed their handguns and asked whether he was there to "commit an act of violence or as part of a 'jihad,'" according to a statement by the American Civil Liberties Union, which is also representing Fatihah.

Ironically, the Muslim ban, which was theoretically conceived by its bigoted creators in order to keep people safe, caused serious injury to a man who, while *protecting* the Save Yourself Survival Gun Range from potential Muslim customers, accidentally dropped his weapon and shot himself, calling to mind natural selection.

"There is no justification for a business denying people service based on religion," Fatihah said. "I am a servant of my community in every respect, and as a proud American, I have enlisted in the U.S. Army Reserve to protect this country. I should be afforded the same rights and privileges as anyone else."

In 2015 CAIR filed a similar lawsuit against Andy Hallinan, owner of Florida Gun Supply in Inverness, Florida, who also declared his gun store a *Muslim-Free Zone* by posting the proclamation in his store window.

"I don't give a fuck what people think about me. I'm going to say it how I believe it is," Hallinan told me. "In my opinion—how the terrorists win—is they get people like me to shut up. To sit down, get afraid of lawsuits, and shut up. That's not the way we need to do it in this country."

In addition to his headline-making sign, Hallinan also became notorious nationwide for the Confederate flag art fund-raiser he organized with another infamous Floridian, George Zimmerman, the former neighborhood watch guy who shot a young African-American, Trayvon Martin, to death.

"There are plenty of gun shops in America. You don't have to bother mine," Hallinan added. "I care about my community. I care about my family. I want to make sure that who I put a gun in front of is not going to use it to harm somebody in my community."

In its federal lawsuit the Florida chapter of CAIR argued that Hallinan's store policy amounted to religious discrimination and violated the Civil Rights Act of 1964. But the claim was later dismissed by a U.S. district judge, ruling that CAIR, who had filed the suit on behalf of its members, lacked standing since the suit did not name a specific plaintiff that was harmed.

Though Hallinan won his case, he has paid the price in other ways: his ex-wife is trying to strip him of custody rights to his kids, and he has received unwanted backlash. "I get death threats every day," he said. "It's bullshit. Listen, I mean, here in America, we have the right to refuse business to anyone we deem a threat—for any reason. Radical Islamic extremists don't believe that you exist on this planet—and that your life isn't as valuable as theirs—and it's their job to kill in the name of their intolerant religion."

As of December 2017, Fatihah was still awaiting his day in court, and Laizure felt optimistic about CAIR's case against the Oklahoma gun range. Unlike the case against Hallinan, CAIR's plaintiff, Fatihah, did "suffer injury from being denied the services of the establishment."

Furthermore, Laizure said that the law is clear. "Under Title II of the Civil Rights Act, it's illegal for a business to discriminate against who can use your service ... based on religion or race or national origin," she said. "That is where they violate the law."

This type of discrimination has happened before. "It's unfortunately similar to what we've historically seen with public business accommodations in the South during the 1960s that literally advertised black people weren't allowed," Laizure added.

The American Freedom Law Center, the same legal counsel that represented Hallinan, is defending the Oklahoma gun range. The firm is run by David Yerushalmi, the very same David Yerushalmi who spoke via Skype at the ACT for America meeting that I paid twenty dollars to attend and is an esteemed member of the Southern Poverty Law Center's hate group watch list.

"This is a setup, and that's what we're seeing," Hallinan concluded. "If this business said, 'Only Muslims allowed' ... we would have half of America cheering for them."

Still, Laizure and her colleagues believe that the law is on their side—and hope the suit will send a message to any other store owners who feel emboldened by Trump to institute their own Muslim bans.

"We're hoping [Fatihah's case] will show American Muslims that they have the right to be served at businesses and not to be denied service because of their religion," Laizure said. "We're hoping that this case will establish more religious protection for Muslim Americans under Title II. And we're hoping that this will have implications for other establishments that have decided to declare themselves to be Muslim-free in violation of federal civil rights law."

In the meantime Hallinan, Keller, Jan Morgan, and Save Yourself Survival Gun Range continue to echo—one handgun at a time—the Trump anthem that there's no time for political correctness or rights for certain American citizens.

A MATCH MADE IN HEAVEN

PART THREE

INTRODUCTION

DON'T WORRY, TRUMP IS TOAST

O F THE MANY CURIOUS political alignments and alliances that resulted in Trump's win, one of those remarked upon with exceptional expressions of surprise was the decision of "family values" Christian conservatives to endorse and support the Republican nominee. Donald Trump, after all, was hardly the embodiment of a God-fearing man who conformed to their ideal president. He was thrice married, with both divorces occurring as the direct result of infidelity (his). He was famous for cutting corners in his business, engaging in such dishonest business practices as not paying for work completed by his building contractors. And those businesses! Gambling casinos where prostitutes ply their trade. Gaudy monuments to Mammon.

What did people like the son of Jerry "Moral Majority" Falwell, who runs Liberty University, see in Donald Trump, a man who may never have darkened the inside of a house of worship prior to his campaign advisors' explanations that he couldn't win the GOP nomination without the support of the Christian Right?

The answer, of course, is that many of these Christians are not actual dictionary-definition Christians, as in people who would happily give up everything they have to follow Christ and his teachings. They are cultural Christians who identify with the Republican Party. This isn't because the Republican Party is Christian, or that there's much overlap between Christianity and contemporary Republicanism. It's because these are "Christians" who see Christianity as white, right-wing, nationalist, and radically opposed to modernity, progressivism, and individual freedoms that threaten their hegemony.

Cultural conservatives always vote Republican. Republican voters always support the Republican nominee. Donald Trump was that nominee, so they supported him. The wonder, to the extent that there is one, is that they supported him enthusiastically. This, I think, can largely—if not entirely—be explained by Christian conservatives' desires to see their conservative values and policy preferences promoted aggressively. Whatever else he was to them, Donald Trump was aggressive. As Trump advisor Steve Bannon marveled, Trump was like that viral honey badger video: he just didn't care what anyone thought about what he said or did. They loved that.

These forces aligned in broad daylight. Many commentators remarked upon them. Still, most of the coastal pundit class couldn't understand that they were important, even determinative. They didn't know right-wingers, especially not Christian right-wingers—not personally anyway. So they couldn't internalize that they were legion—and that their vast numbers and wild enthusiasm could make a real difference in a national election.

Unlike many of my colleagues, I knew Trump would probably win. But there's one thing I never saw coming. I didn't know he was a far-right extremist.

Who would have ever thought that a president would defend Nazis and Klansmen—repeatedly, even after catching hell for doing so? That, to appease "very fine" Nazis and Klansmen, a president wouldn't bother to phone the family of a high-profile political murder? (Trump waited four days to call—and first did so during her funeral.) That a president of the United States would elevate the leaders of the defeated, treasonous Confederacy to the level of America's Founding Fathers?

As CNN's Anderson Cooper observed after Trump's now-infamous news conference, "A few hours ago, the President of the United States revealed to us so clearly who he really is."

Who is he?

At best, an enabler and apologist for fascists.

At worst, a fascist himself. Though, to be fair, comparing Trump to fascists is unfair to fascists. Fascists got things done: infrastructure, for example.

There were plenty of signs of Trump's fascist tendencies. He promised to bring back torture. He approvingly recounted an incredibly (i.e., literally untrue) racist story that U.S. occupation troops executed Muslim Filipino patriots with bullets dipped in pig's blood. He repeatedly encouraged violence against peaceful liberal protesters at his rallies. He "joked" that cops ought to bash suspects' heads into the sides of squad cars. And he wants to refill the infamous concentration camp at Guantánamo.

During the campaign there were also indications that Trump might be a reasonable man. Gay Republicans assured us his White House would respect pro-LGBTQIA rights. During the campaign, Trump said Caitlyn Jenner should feel free to use the Trump Tower bathroom of her choice. Strange to think about now, but this is the same guy who endorsed single-payer healthcare, called for a tax increase on the wealthy, promised to lay off Planned Parenthood, and came out for amnesty for illegal immigrants— albeit after deporting them and then letting them back in (to help out the airlines, maybe?).

Candidate Trump was satisfyingly over the place.

President Trump has been terrifyingly consistent.

Nixon, Reagan, and George W. Bush appointed Democrats to top posts. Not Trump. His cabinet and top staff is composed of rabid right-wing lily-white ideologues; it features more generals than an old-school junta. Trump's first major policy initiatives—repealing Obamacare (with no replacement) and tax cuts for the rich—have tilted so far right that he can't even secure the support of the usual sellout Vichy Democrats or so-called "moderate" Republicans.

Even by the standards of a country whose citizens—even the "liberal" ones—believe that they have the right to invade and bomb any country they feel like without justification, Trump's presser and ensuing tweets were truly special.

"Mainstream" Republicans, such as Mitch McConnell, may have the souls of Nazis. But actual Nazism—the uniforms, the flags, the crazy rune shields—is not done by Americans. Actual Nazism is reserved for a few thousand pasty, tattoo-covered muscleheads with little pig eyes. They are freaks. They are few. Yet they have a friend in this president.

Let's be clear: there isn't much ideological daylight between "mainstream" Republicanism and little-pig-eyed Nazism. Nazism is militarily expansionist; so is U.S. foreign policy (which, to be fair, is equally supported by Democrats). Nazism centers around a dynamic cult of the Leader; Republicans rally around their president no matter what outlandish crap gets vomited out by his mouth. Nazism relies on scapegoating and hearkens to a mythic past when the nation was united by a common cause and everyone—everyone who matters—was happier and more prosperous (c.f. **Make America Great Again** and Republicans' baseless claims that illegal immigrants are criminals and rapists).

So Trump's defense of Nazis and Klansmen isn't a radical departure from the GOP political norm. Where he's gone off the rails by American standards is a question of style.

Trump's manner—aptly described by Senator Bob Corker as a lack of "steadiness" and "competence"—is why he almost certainly will not complete his term.

Racism isn't the issue—Republicanism is racist. It's a matter of decorum.

Trump is too tacky, high-strung, and unpredictable for the business class. America's ruling elites like their racism served up quietly in a well-tailored suit, under a tight helmet of elder-statesman hair, delivered calmly and slowly, so bland that no one pays attention.

This is where Mike Pence comes in.

Even the Christian fundamentalists won't see what already seems obvious: it's hard to imagine Donald Trump completing a full term as president. But they will love Mike Pence. He may not be a honey badger. But he is one of them.

–**Ted Rall**

Speaking of Christian fundamentalists, **Harmon** infiltrates some...

CHAPTER 8

BEST LITTLE HELL HOUSE IN TEXAS

THE ACTRESS WHO WAS to be shot in the face inside the domestic violence room proclaimed, "If the gun doesn't work, we assume Jesus knows why!" She then gathered her fellow cast members in hope that they would lend a hand in ensuring that the prop gun worked, thus making the murder scene more effective: "We are going to pray over the gun and have Jesus fix whatever is wrong with it!"

And pray they did. Hallelujah!

Throughout a series of makeshift structures behind the suburban Texas megachurch, everyone prepped for the evening ahead. Teens practiced screaming. Volunteers applied makeup to demons. In the abortion room the team worked on blocking moves for the actress who would be thrown to the floor. And the guy who portrayed the unwed dad lounged on the couch, wearing headphones and playing Candy Crush on his iPhone.

"We're shorthanded in the abortion room. I'm either going to put you in there or drunk driving," said Brother Thomas, who wore a military cap blazoned with *God's Army*.

"The abortion room would be great!" I replied, feeling mildly uncomfortable since as a grown man I was much older than the rest of the volunteers, who were all teenagers.

"When they come in—what I need you to do—is yell in a strong voice, 'Watch the steps,'" he instructed, before informing me that if we didn't tell people to watch their step and they fell, then we were legally liable.

At Hell House Jesus apparently had his limits. He could steer kids towards the Lord, but he couldn't prevent—or indemnify—lawsuits.

For those unfamiliar with the ways of the Bible Belt, a Hell House is the right-wing Christian alternative to the standard-issue Halloween haunted house. But instead of Freddy Krueger jumping out of the shadows and scaring the living bejesus out of you, these costumed evangelists tried to scare the holy Jesus into you.

This Halloween Trojan Horse is designed to frighten pre-teen kids into religion and steer them directly into the sweet salvation of evangelical Christianity—lest these evil sinners suffer the consequences!

Hell House volunteers shepherd various youth groups through a series of horrific "real-life" scenes that have been designed to create terror and revulsion. For example, in this house of horrors, being gay inevitably results in a painful ugly death from AIDS, and engaging in premarital sex leads the homecoming queen down a slippery slope into drugs and prostitution.

Outreach manuals helpfully include tips on how to create authentic abortion room scenes: "Purchase a meat product that closely resembles pieces of a baby to be placed in a glass bowl." Holy fuck!?! If you know what "pieces of baby" look like, then you should probably be in prison.

At the end, Hell House patrons are asked to accept salvation—by repenting their sins and trusting in Jesus Christ—or face an eternity in Hell, which is graphically and entertainingly depicted in the final Hell House scene.

The largest Hell House in the country—produced by Trinity Church in Cedar Hill, Texas (a Dallas suburb)—was depicted in the classic 2002 documentary film *Hell House*, which featured many horrific scenes, including one where a girl spewed vats of blood from her vagina-region after an abortion.

Fifteen thousand people, mostly Christians who would become Trump supporters (eighty-one percent of evangelicals voted for him), were expected to pass through the God-fearing gates of the twenty-third annual event, whose theme was ***Darkness Has a Name.***

The website warned visitors: "There are guns, blood, violence, intense scenes, and disturbing images." I wondered what horrors *sinners* would face in the staged scenes. Would twerking cause someone to catch AIDS and suffer a ghastly death? Would posting sexy selfies compel Satan's wrath?

It was time to experience Hell from the inside. I emailed Trinity Church and requested a volunteer form. My concocted backstory explained that I was a lost soul who had rededicated his life to Jesus after years of abusing crank. Like Travis Bickle in the movie *Taxi Driver*, I stressed: "I'm available to do any position that's needed. I could work next weekend and the weekend after and the weekend after that ..."

Fortunately, Hell House didn't do an NSA background check. An organizer emailed me back: "I will use you as a tour guide or in the prayer room. Just come on out next weekend, and I'll get you plugged in."

Done! I purchased a plane ticket to Texas and flew off to the world of Hell House. Help me, Jesus. Help me!

"Get them in and get them out—and on to the next group," announced the team leader as a massive line queued up outside the Trinity Church choir room. Each attendee had plopped down twelve dollars for a ticket, and it was show time for bad amateur religious theatrics performed by teenagers.

I was assigned to the lesbian suicide room. My job was to lead groups from the sex-trafficking area to a high school scene that was being enacted from behind a piece of yellow police caution tape. The premise: after a girl's classmates accused her of being a lesbian, suicide followed.

As this homophobic parable unfolded, a youth group stood shoulder-to-shoulder and watched, transfixed, while a petrified ten-year-old boy tightly clutched his mom's hand.

"Let me tell you about my favorite student, Alex," proclaimed a youth performer, caked with a large bloody gash across his head. "She's grown up pure. She's never had a boyfriend. Never been kissed. She's saving herself for the right man …"

For stereotypical realism, the actress portraying the accused lesbian wore a plaid shirt.

"DON'T TOUCH ME, LESBIAN!" sneered the girl's best friend, who left with a huff, loudly slamming the door behind her. Unable to face a reality where her Christian peers demonized her for being gay, the lead actress killed herself by downing a handful of pills.

"Alex has been pure her whole life. Look what good it did her. Now she'll be with me forever!" sneered the teenager portraying Satan's helper.

Aaaand … scene!

As I quickly steered the solemn youth group towards the drunk-driving room, one of the church leaders—already aware of my Hell House work ethic—remarked to me, "You're doing a good job." I beamed with vocational pride.

He offered me a suggestion to enhance the scene: "When you have groups in here, I want you to pray."

I vigorously nodded my head.

"If you can pray in tongues, even better," he added.

After a moment, I replied, "Okay."

Pray in tongues? How does one even do that ... without laughing? I decided to make rapid gibberish noises with my mouth while throwing in some lyrics from the Styx song "Mr. Roboto."

"MAKE YOUR WAY IN QUICKLY!" I screamed, herding in another youth group. I barked more commands, growing slightly mad with power: "SCOOCH TOGETHER! PEOPLE IN THE MIDDLE, KNEEL DOWN. NOW STAND BACK UP AGAIN. MOVE IN, OR THE DEMONS WILL BE ANGRY!"

The scene began: "Alex, are you a lesbian?"

I summoned a pair of teenagers. "Pray with me!" I demanded, before mumbling, "*Dōmo arigatō*, Mr. Roboto ..."

A small child bolted from one of the Hell House scene rooms and vomited. His mother followed close behind. Throughout the night, other frightened children followed his lead.

As I popped my head into the abortion scene room, I wondered if any famous actors got their starts on the Hell House circuit. Doubtful, since subtlety was not the key here. A cold, uncaring medical staff member was advising a young woman to terminate her pregnancy via an abortion while a red-faced demon with a sarcastic voice taunted her: "Why not have an abortion? Everyone is doing it these days!"

During the scene, a girl in the audience tried to hide her tears, solidifying the fact that the actress portraying "Abortion Girl" was the Queen of the Hell House Ball. Her tour de force performance included hysterically screaming while being thrown to the ground by her angry boyfriend, who, of course, left her forever.

When I returned to my post in the lesbian suicide room, I felt slightly insecure, concerned that my fourteen-year-old Hell House coworkers didn't like me.

Between groups, I asked the satanic demon with the bloody gash in his head: "How many times do you do this a night?"

He responded, "Hundreds of times," as a gunshot erupted from the sex-trafficking room, followed by an actor screaming, "You ARE home, bitch!"

It seemed as if my level of punishment in Dante's Hell included seeing teens reenact, over and over again, the exact same lesbian suicide scene.

A kid, gripping his chest, required assistance mere moments after entering the room. "I can't breathe," he said. Taking a page from *Saving Private Ryan*, I grabbed the kid by the shoulder and quickly assisted him out of Hell House.

"What scared him so much?" I asked a church leader after the ordeal.

"The whole experience," he replied. "He was panicking. He was really freaked out. This all scared him. He was clinging to his mom, and she had a hard time walking through the rooms with him."

The church leader seemed pleased that Hell House was doing its job.

"What if another kid freaks out?" I worriedly asked. "What should I do?"

He assured me that there would be plenty more terrified souls. "Get him out the door and take him to the prayer room," he said. "You're going to have adults doing the same thing. We had seven adults come out of the coffin room last night. We had to take them all down to the decision room."

As his group left the domestic-violence room, a teen in a stocking cap groused, "It was scarier last year." And regarding the schoolroom shooting scene, staged fresh on the heels of Sandy Hook, he noted, "In the past, they scared us into reality. Now they are making us think about making the right decisions."

He might have thought that these scenes represented a kinder, gentler Hell House, but the potential for emotional and psychological trauma remained.

Take, for example, the Hell House radio ads, in which a Monster Truck Rally voice invited people to "come see the funeral of a homosexual AIDS patient." Fred Phelps applauded from his grave!

Sure, Hell House might lead more kids to church pews. But what about the children it psychologically damages by convincing them that being gay or having sex before marriage is a ticket straight to hell?

After witnessing an actor shoot his fictional son and strangle his fictional wife (bad things that the church believes the children must see), a chubby kid went into shock: his face turned white as a sheet, and he sweated profusely.

"Just stick by my side," Brother Thomas instructed the traumatized child, before turning to the youth pastor and saying, "We're about to go into the coffin room. I'll keep him close to the exit in case he needs to leave."

This poor kid was going to shit his Jesus-fearing pants when he entered the next room and got stuffed into a makeshift coffin with shrieking demons pounding on its sides.

Inside this dark and claustrophobic room, a video displayed graphic scenes from Mel Gibson's *The Passion of the Christ* as a ghoulish voice commanded visitors to climb inside one of the several oversized upright wall coffins.

I was crammed, with three scared teenagers, into one of the caskets. But they needn't fear. I was there to help, praying, "*Dōmo arigatō*, Mr. Roboto …"

We were now in Hell, where human sacrifice took place and masked ghouls and demons taunted—with horrific shrieks and screams—those who were in the room. Smaller children clung to their parents in fear. Hey sinners! Welcome to your future!

When the youth groups emerged from Hell, they were greeted by the "cool" pastor. In the brightly-lit decision room, he jumped up on a chair and played the role of good cop to Hell House's bad cop.

"If you want your get out of Hell free card, it's your connection to God himself," said the cool pastor. "We want to introduce you to the King himself. We want to get you hooked on God. That is our purpose here in Hell House. We're going to open the door. Do what God tells you to do. The only way out is if you want to go in and pray!"

At first, only one child entered the prayer room. Then, everyone else followed. What other option did these kids have? Either pray, or it's back to the Hell room—for eternity! No one wanted to be the devil's bidet.

The Decision Room played out like a scene from *Glengarry Glen Ross*. Youth group members were required to sign forms—keeping it legally binding—that stated their commitment to Jesus Christ.

A prayer counselor spoke in tongues—but did it for "real"—as he wrapped his hands around two kids. "You're amazing, oh God. You're amazing," he prayed. "There's nothing the enemy can do to bind us anymore. You kneel for me in front of my enemy. In the name of Jesus, Amen."

One of the kids observed, "Wow. That was intense."

Culminating the drama, God's wrath came thundering down in the form of a huge, Texas-size lightning storm. Hail and rain poured from the heavens and thumped off the tin roofs of the Hell House buildings. Soaking-wet audience members continued to navigate through the procession and onto the next Passion Play.

In order to be heard over the thumping storm, tired child actors screamed their lines. "I'M SO DRUNK!" could be heard bellowing from the drunk-driving room as people strained to hear what the hell else was being said. The demons looked exhausted.

"If the lights go out, don't panic," advised Brother Thomas. "Let me know if water is coming close to any of the electrical equipment."

It seemed as though lightning would come crashing through the roof and erupt the lesbian suicide scene into flames. Raindrops from the ceiling fell on stage, and water dripped down the walls like blood in *The Amityville Horror*.

It was the end of days.

Awesome.

CHAPTER 9

HE BLINDED ME WITH BIBLICAL SCIENCE

INVITING A CREATIONIST AND A SCIENTIST TO DISCUSS EVOLUTION ISN'T DEBATE— IT'S SOPHISTRY. THERE AREN'T "TWO SIDES" TO GLOBAL WARMING: SCIENTISTS AGREE THAT'S IT'S A FACT. FOR FUN, LET'S TAKE A LOOK AT WHAT TV WOULD LOOK LIKE IF "BOTH SIDES" OF THE ISSUES WERE *TRULY* REPRESENTED:

THE ARGUMENT CAME DOWN to those goddamn forty-three hundred-year-old dinosaur bones—the very bones of our ancestors' purported playmates. "No one is going to convince me the word of God is not true. No one is going to tell me the flood is not true," stated Ken Ham to a crowd of nine hundred spectators who hung on to his every word.

According to Ham, dinosaur fossils are remnants of Noah's biblical flood, and to him, that's an historical and scientific fact. "Kids aren't being taught critically or correctly!" he sternly proclaimed.

"Show me one piece of evidence, and I would change my mind immediately," retorted Ham's opponent, a bow tie-sporting scientist who madly waved his arms.

I looked around the room, hoping to catch eyes with someone to whom I could give the knowing wink—the secret handshake of sanity—that confirmed Ham's "science" was complete bullshit. Sadly, within this hall of citizens, who were clad mostly in Bill Cosby sweaters, that solace was nowhere to be found.

At this self-promoted "super debate" in Kentucky, where science was pitted head-to-head against a fairy tale, the exchanges were about to become heated. In one corner, natural history. And in the other corner, an invisible masculine deity who created everything. So much was on the line in this battle between the Big Bang theory and the creation myth, which holds that around six thousand years ago God created the universe (and everything in it) in six literal (not metaphorical) days.

Scientific consensus, however, teaches us that the universe, as it now appears, began approximately thirteen billion eight hundred million years ago with the Big Bang, a massive explosion of energy and matter. Over nine billion years later, the earth was formed from a cloud of dust and gas known as a solar nebula.

The direct lineage of *Homo sapiens*, or human beings, can be traced back roughly two million years. Civilization, the human settlements that sprung up in Mesopotamia about ten to fifteen thousand years ago after some people abandoned hunter-gathering in favor of agriculture, predates recorded history, which corresponds with the advent of cuneiform script by the Sumerians approximately three thousand five hundred years prior to the alleged birth of Christ.

But not all Americans accept this history. A 2017 Pew poll found that thirty-four percent believe the Biblical view of creation by God and reject the science that life on earth, including humans, evolved over time.

Not since the "good ol' days"—when citizens gathered in a Tennessee courtroom to watch the trial of a science teacher, who was charged criminally for teaching Darwinism to his public school students—was a Southern audience so excited.

The sixty-five-year-old Australian-born pied piper of biblical literalism, Ken Ham, was set to defend creationism in a battle of wits against the free world's defender of evolution, Bill Nye the Science Guy (apparently, the Mythbusters gents were busy). Move over Galileo, Descartes, Francis Bacon, and Hugh Miller. Make room for Bill Nye, who—after appearing on *Dancing with the Stars*—had chosen to go *mano a mano* with creationist Ham in this media-frenzy-spectacle that would have made Carl Sagan weep.

Yes, it had come to this: the culture war as live entertainment. It was red state versus blue state—WWE-style. Go, logic!

I was headed to Petersburg, Kentucky—home of the famous and unaccredited Creation museum—to witness "young earth creationist" Ken Ham duke it out for God's army. With my camera charged and two pens and a new notebook in tow, I was about to witness a debate on evolution staged in front of a crowd of non-believing science skeptics. How could this NOT be a good night out?

As my rental-car radio scanned a roulette of Jesus-oriented stations, I spotted a brown road sign that hearkened the exit to the Creation Museum, where humans are presented Flintstones-style, living contemporaneously with dinosaurs.

An hour and a half before the big Showdown at the Garden of Eden Corral, the parking lot was already a sea of cars and TV production trucks. A nervous buzz, like in *Waiting for Guffman*, resonated throughout the complex, where visitors were asked to respect the ideas expressed within its hallowed grounds, i.e., please don't openly mock the insanity. The Creation Museum's motto, "Prepare to Believe," sounded like the tagline of a Criss Angel magic illusion show.

"Are you excited about tonight's debate?" I asked a motherly volunteer at the door.

"We're not supposed to talk about it," she said from inside the seventy-thousand-square-foot hall of misinformation, where kids can have their photos taken while riding a lifelike, animatronic dinosaur. "We want to make sure we get all the information right."

The superhero match-up of this debate, which was live-streamed into schools around the country, had been brewing since Bill Nye posted to YouTube the video "Creationism Is Not Appropriate for Children." At the time of the debate, it had garnered over seven million views.

Security for the debate was intense: attendees passed a row of uniformed sheriffs and bomb-sniffing dogs before going through TSA-style metal detectors and a weapons pat-down.

"Why all the security and the security dogs?" I asked a uniformed guard while thinking to myself, "Aren't religious fanatics only supposed to bomb abortion clinics?"

He curtly replied, "I really can't go into those reasons."

As we, the esteemed media, were whisked past fantastical river scenes (of dinosaurs and children gleefully playing together) and led into a small room for a pre-debate press conference with evolution-denier Ken Ham, the press liaison announced, "Mr. Nye has not arrived. So, he will not be accessible to the media."

After a few awkward moments, Ham—a former public school science teacher and current conservative religious icon—emerged to face the mainstream media and confront a myriad of microphones and cameras. Clad in casual garb, Ham exhibited signs of pre-debate jitters.

The floor opened for questions. Fortunately, I was able to contain myself from asking Ham: "Will you crucify Bill Nye in tonight's debate?" Now, don't get me wrong. I'm not just mocking Ken Ham for his beliefs on human origins; I'm also mocking him for his creepy stances on homosexuality and sibling marriage—yes, he thinks brothers and sisters should be allowed to marry. Plus, he believes evolutionary thought is the culprit behind secular government, feminism, and moral relativism, all of which he despises.

In Ham's view, if even one singular point in the Bible is compromised, then the whole house of cards will tumble down until daily life in America resembles a San Francisco gay pride parade.

"I tried to think how Bill Nye thinks," Ham stated when asked about debate preparation. "I did a lot of thinking and praying and asked God for a lot of wisdom." Thus far, God did not seem to have granted his wish.

"What do you think Nye's approach will be?" posed another astute reporter, giving Ham the pregame third-degree.

"One of his major points—if you teach children creationism and not evolution, you're going to undermine technology," said Ham, not knowing what to do with his arms. "Some of the secularists have tried to shut down the discussion of origins in schools. If evolution is fact, like the secularists are saying, then why would they be afraid of us debating with them in public?"

He answered his own question: "I think they're worried. They know that if we actually give information to people who previously didn't have access to it, they will start to think that maybe the Bible could be true!"

So, what is really at stake? Taxpayer dollars being used to fund the teaching of creationism—passed off as scientific fact—in public schools. Over eighty-two million taxpayer dollars have been distributed to schools in Texas, Arkansas, and Indiana to promote this myth to kids: God—in a magical, enchanted garden inhabited by a talking serpent—created Eve, the first woman, from the rib he had taken out of Adam, the first man.

Then a meddling reporter crapped into Ham's creationist pool: "It's been said that the debate is good timing on your part due to the funding needed for the Ark park." At the time, Ham's Utopian construction of a scale-model Noah's Ark had been temporarily halted due to a lack of funds. "With the publicity from this event, how would you react to people who would cynically say that's what this debate is all about?"

Ham snapped, "It has nothing to do with the funding of the Ark."

The reporter continued, "Can you talk about the funding of the Ark park and its status?"

Ham retorted, "We're under strict instructions not to talk about it!" Why? And from whom?

"Thanks for coming," abruptly blurted the press liaison. "There will be someone here to escort you into Legacy Hall."

And boom. Drop the mic. Media questioning over!

Three weeks later, Ham would announce that the debate had spurred bond sales and raised enough money to begin construction of the ark. The Ark Encounter opened in 2016.

With over seventy news outlets in attendance, media space was at a premium. "Hey guy, that's my spot," bellowed an overweight cameraman from the *Cincinnati Enquirer,* who was way too possessive over his small corner of the large, packed auditorium. Rows and rows of cameras were poised at the stage, which was littered with bookshelves and pictures of dinosaurs. With such media fanfare, one might expect a surprise visit from Sarah Palin riding in on a winged unicorn. "This should make the front page of the Cincinnati paper," boasted the cameraman's assistant.

The Fox News reporter delivered his pre-debate remote as though it were a big story that would transform history. This just in ... the earth is only six thousand years old!

"Is this a big news event for you?" I asked a TV cameraman, who looked like Phillip Seymour Hoffman.

"This is more of a sporting event," he smirked.

As the refrigerator-white audience filtered into the auditorium, heroic, New Age music—the soundtrack to a PowerPoint slide that read **Biology. Sociology. Astronomy. Archeology. Geology.**—reverberated. A video of Bill Nye—explaining how giraffes developed long necks due to natural selection—played on two large monitors, apparently designed to rile the hostile creationist crowd and paint

Nye as the heel.

"The Bible says God created man. It doesn't say evolved," a woman told a reporter. "I really believe those who believe in evolution will have their eyes opened tonight!"

Amongst the crowd of creationists, I spotted a few bow tie-clad Bill Nye disciples rooting for science over hocus-pocus.

As start time approached, the New Age music intensified, and the packed room became deathly silent. The debate, scheduled to last two and a half hours, began with opening statements and was followed by thirty-minute presentations, rebuttals, counter-rebuttals, and a preselected audience Q&A that discussed whether the earth is four billion five hundred million years old or only six thousand. The discrepancy between the two numbers is a factor of seven hundred fifty thousand; it would be like stating that the distance from San Francisco to New York is twenty-one feet instead of three thousand miles.

"We know there are people who disagree with each other in this room," advised a debate spokesman. "Please, no cheering or disruptive behavior."

CNN's Tom Foreman emerged from darkness, plucked out of Wolf Blitzer's Situation Room, to act as the debate moderator. Enter Nye. Enter Ham. The two shook hands, and the coin was tossed. Ham won. Divine intervention, perhaps? It was time to strap in for a long, crazy ride and party like it was 1899!

"The world of science has been hijacked by secular scientists," Ham said as he punched up various PowerPoint slides and graphs. Most of his sentences began with, "Here's another important fact," and in an apparent attempt to legitimize the Bible, he said "science" more times than a drunken pirate says "shiver me timbers."

Ham even claimed to have "evidence confirming God's word" but never presented it. Instead, he read from a list the names of obscure, rogue scientists who believed in creationism while slides attempted to show that these scientists, in fact, did exist. Pointing to one of the scientist's photo, Ham proclaimed, "He's a creationist JUST LIKE I AM!" To Ham, these scientists were the victims of creationismphobia: "They're afraid to speak out in fear of being criticized by the media."

While Ham explained how the Grand Canyon was formed in a few thousand years, Nye—as composed as an emotionless wax dummy—stared on and dug deep into his personal cave.

When it was his turn, Nye opened with a joke about bow ties before stupefying the crowd with a simplified explanation of why the world wasn't created by a handful of magic beans on the back of a giant tortoise while Apollo crossed the sky on a fiery chariot.

Attempting to speak to the masses on their own terms, he equated evolution to something you'd see on one of those crime scene TV shows. "Trust clues from the past to help solve the mysteries of creation," stated Nye as a slide with photos of various *CSI* actors appeared on the hall's large screens.

Quicker than you could say "Scopes Monkey Trial," Nye added with confidence, "We are standing on millions of layers of ancient life. How could those animals have lived their entire life, and formed these layers, in just four thousand years?"

For the most part, the audience looked glossy-eyed, with arms tightly folded and facial expressions that read, "Don't try and fool us with your trickery, TV science man!"

"When it comes to the past, you don't see a dinosaur bone with a tag that says how old it is," rebutted Ham with simplified logic. "There's an infallible dating method and that's from someone who was there. And that was God! The Bible is the world of God!"

For the next two hours, Nye and Ham argued over tree rings, ice core samples, the distance of the stars from earth, and vegetarian lions. At one point, they discussed whether or not the Biblical flood actually happened and debated the existence of Noah's four hundred fifty feet long wooden ark. Think of it this way: in 2014, more than six hundred people became deathly ill as norovirus spread throughout the passengers and crew on a week-long Royal Caribbean cruise. If such a thing could happen on a modern cruise ship, then imagine the horrendous sanitation standards of a biblical boat, which stayed afloat for a year, filled with animals packed tighter than caged foie gras geese.

This visual image might be funny if it were coming from one man screaming at the midday sun. But these myths—global floods, virgin births, magical resurrections, and humans living with dinosaurs—are the scientific beliefs of a large cross-section of Americans who demand that their religious fantasies be taught in public schools.

"There's a book out there that explains that," Ham said. "The first line is 'In the beginning.'" The crowd laughed, and he used the same line two more times throughout the evening. The third time, however, failed to muster a smile from the captive audience. "It's the only theory that makes logical sense."

After a while, the familiar creationist patter became boring as Ham tried to poke holes in carbon-dating techniques, claiming that the method is not provable, even though it's been developed through observation, validation, and repetition.

As the evening progressed, he brought up more Bible stories and expected them to be accepted carte blanche—with, of course, zero evidence—because they appear in the Bible.

When all else failed, Ham simply threw out: "God did it!" He used the phrase as if it were his get-out-of-jail-free card.

At the conclusion of his arguments, I almost expected to hear the picking of a banjo. Nye, you've been served!

"I take Genesis as literal history. We're teaching the kids the right way to think," Ham said. Now near the end of the evening, his voice shook, and his body language revealed a sense of insecurity as a result of Nye's scientific onslaught.

"I'm completely unsatisfied!" retorted Nye as grumbling erupted amongst Ham's followers. "Mr. Ham, what can you prove? Is Ken's creationist model viable?" he asked the audience. "I say absolutely not."

Satisfied, a pro-science posse—wearing T-shirts that proclaimed **Bill Nye Is My Homeboy**—abruptly left the auditorium, intentionally missing Ham's finale. "There's a book out there called the Bible," he said. "It tells us all the origins. If the book is really true—it should explain the world."

Ham, like any true capitalist, then invited everyone to exit through the gift shop and pre-order DVD copies of the night's debate for only $15.99.

As the audience spilled out, the leader of the *Bill Nye Is My Homeboy* posse contemplated what he just saw: "The facts of science are on the side of evolution. There's a lot missing in creationism delivered as literal truth."

A posse member added, "You have one side that presents facts and the other side that presents a world-view based on personal beliefs. When it comes to science, and what we teach in our schools, clearly one side beats out the other."

Conversely, a mustached man shared with me his belief that Bill Nye couldn't explain everything. "However, a book is written that has all the answers to the mystery," he said. "So what do you believe? Do you believe man, or do you believe God? The word of God is true!"

Perhaps it shouldn't have been surprising that this debate settled nothing. When one side operates from a foundational truth—that the Bible was written by God and is therefore gospel—nothing, including facts, can change their minds. For the other side, blind faith isn't in their vernacular. This issue isn't one of those agree-to-disagree things. The intellectual chasm between the two sides is baked into this rhetorical cake.

If Ham had his way, kids would stop staring at the stars and contemplating how to solve the mysteries of the universe. For him, all scientific pondering is unnecessary; everything can be explained with three simple words: "God did it!"

As we were exiting the building, a uniformed sheriff announced, "There's a Level Two weather emergency." It was an ice storm.

Ken Ham would say that the ice storm—and other catastrophic weather events—is God's retribution against man for Adam's original sin in the Garden of Eden. At least when the big flood arrives, he'll have his very own Noah's Ark replica in which he can sail away from his unaccredited museum, leaving behind the doubting Bill Nyes of the world, two by two at a time.

CHAPTER 10
IT'S A PURITY RING THANG

HUNDREDS OF AWKWARD TEENAGERS were gathered in a large auditorium in Cincinnati. If all went as planned, not a single soul in attendance would have sex before marriage. "This ring is a visual reminder of your commitment," said Spence, the cool youth leader utilizing street talk to connect with the teens. "I want you to keep it on—and not take off, you understand—until your wedding night."

As he spoke, Spence periodically turned his hip-hop baseball cap backwards and then forwards. He instructed everyone to stand up and directed their attention to the large multimedia screens directly behind him.

"Yo! The very last thing," Spence said, keeping it realz, "what you see on screen is a vow—it's a verbal commitment to God. I'm going to start us off, and we're all going to read it out loud. Here we go ..."

There were no smiles; everyone was taking this ritual seriously, except me.

The teenagers chanted in unison:

In signing this covenant before God Almighty, I agree to wear a silver ring as a sign of my pledge to abstain from sexual behavior that is inconsistent with Biblical standards. On my wedding day, I will present my silver ring to my spouse, representing my faithful commitment to the marriage covenant.

At the conclusion of the vow, Spence screamed, "CLAP YOUR HANDS!!" The thunderous applause of hundreds of self-declared virgins echoed throughout the auditorium. "People just met God. Heaven is freaking out. LET'S MAKE SOME NOIZE!"

I was at Cincinnati Christian University for the last leg of the ten-month-long Silver Ring Thing (SRT) – One Night Stand tour: the Cirque du Soleil of Christian teen abstinence programs. Since 1996, their mission has been to convince kids to take the pledge during a mass purity-ring event and abstain from sex before marriage.

At the registration area, hyper teens checked in while youth leaders measured their fingers for silver rings to be picked up after the event. (They really pushed those rings.)

According to adult SRT leaders, teens are dealing with a lot of shame and guilt over sex—most likely instilled by their church leaders and parents constantly bombarding them with the notion that sex is a sin. As a result, nearly five hundred thousand teenagers have attended past SRT shows. The group claims that almost two hundred thousand have put on the silver ring and that eighty-five thousand have given their lives to Christ.

In an attempt to fit in, I was wearing the T-shirt of a local sports team. (There's nothing strange about that guy. He likes local sports!)

I approached a smiling youth leader, flashed for validation my silver purity ring I bought off the Internet (hopefully, I can unload it on eBay afterwards), and said, "I'm here for the parent session." The pre-event—*How will your child navigate the next 5, 10, or 15 years of sexual pressure?*—was to educate parents on how to keep their children's virginity intact.

"I want you to strongly consider putting on a ring yourself—so you can pray for your child's abstinence every day," said a middle-aged man to a room filled with dozens of concerned parents. "How cool (*creepy* might be a better word) is that? I've been wearing this ring for almost fifteen years now. I pray for my daughters' purity every day—all three of them!"

I nodded in agreement. After all, I was just a lone man, on my own, looking concerned about teen virginity and contemplating the visual imagery of a middle-aged man praying for the purity of his daughters. No unrealistically high expectations here; we were just a bunch of adults—who (possibly) have regular sex—relaying to children that vigorous praying and a cheap ring will replace basic human biological needs.

"I wish every parent in America would be doing what you are doing here tonight," the Silver Ring Thing man said, recommending that parents should act as the NSA and monitor their kids' social networks, watch what their kids wear ("don't advertise what you're not selling"), and forbid one-on-one dating until they're sixteen. But even then, he claimed it was necessary to "inform both dating parties what will and will not be acceptable!"

The grown man beamed the benefits of this magical Jesus-controlled chastity belt: "Imagine your kid walking out of the house—to go on a date—and you know that they have a ring on their finger ... and that they value it." The crowd, who apparently viewed the Bible as both a history and medical journal, knowingly nodded in agreement.

Since SRT is Christ-centric, its agenda involves lying to kids about safe sex practices. For example, it claims, "Teenagers' access to condoms has never been greater, yet we have a record number of infections ..."

What about rubbing the genie as a safer alternative to sex? Nope. "The immoral person sins against his own body," the man said. "That's why you'll see so many of them ask God for forgiveness and put on this ring and say, 'I'm done with that.'"

Wow! Being sexually active used to mean having sex with someone else. But for these people in this day and age, sexually active can mean having sex with ... yourself.

"In our schools, there is such a thing they teach called safe sex," he continued with disdain. "But that simply is not true!"

This man told the crowd that evolution-loving public schools instruct students to "respect yourself and your partner enough every time you have sex." Scornful laughter erupted. "That's a value they teach that I think most parents don't agree with." More people nodded. "They say, 'Everyone deserves sexual fulfillment regardless of age, mental capacity, marital status, and sexual preference—as long as the sex is consensual ..."

Parents frowned. (I frowned.) Too bad these people didn't frown when they would later vote for and elect as the leader of the free world a man who advocates grabbing women by the va-jay-jay.

But for these people, Trump's tiny and wandering hands weren't the problem; it was the secular media and its supposed promotion of birth control over abstinence. "Let me tell you about the 'con' in 'condoms,' and the tragic message the media gives our children: 'If you use a condom, you will be protected.'" After a dramatic pause, he concluded, "Nothing can be further than the truth ..."

Before heading to the main event, The Silver Ring Thing's manifesto was revealed:

> *We truly believe what is needed in America is to get back to these intact Christian family structures. If a child has God in them, they have the power to wait; they have the will and God's blessing to pull this off ... It's critical for parents to support and promote an abstinence program in their communities. If we don't do that, we're going to let 'the other voice' get stronger.*

Backed by flashy lights, pumping beats, and glow-sticks, *yo-talking* Spence returned to the stage. "All right! Y'all still with me?" he asked. "Cool. You guys decided to come and kick it with us. And that's awesome!"

So how does the Silver Ring Thing convince these kids to abstain from sex? A two-hour stage performance that incorporates high-energy music, videos, skits, special effects, and "comedy" delivered concert-style so that teenagers can respond and relate.

In addition to devoting their virginity to Christ, these kids got a free glow-stick.

Beside a row of parents, I settled into my chair for a fun evening of Christian abstinence entertainment.

"There's still some people who'd say: 'Dude, you're crazy. There's nobody in my life who'd expect me to wait until I'm married to have sex.'" At this point, I almost expected Spence to drop an n-bomb to try and sound more street, but thankfully, he did not and continued, "I know of one person in your future who does …"

Next, a female volunteer was brought on stage for the classic abstinence skit, *Pieces of My Heart*. A guy held a wooden heart. Each time he broke his purity vow, the wooden heart was also broken, and the pieces were handed to the volunteer, who represented his next *supposed* girlfriend.

"She breaks up with him and breaks a piece of his heart," narrated a SRT team member.

There was more fake sex and more symbolic wooden-heart-breaking. At the end of the skit, a virgin bride appeared: "She waited for you, and what did you do?" The guy looked at his damaged heart and made a sad face: his heart pieces clearly didn't match hers. How, exactly, was this silliness supposed to stop kids—when tangled like mad dogs in the heat of passion—from having sex?

"What part of 'wait until marriage' don't they understand?" I somberly whispered to the mom sitting next to me. She nodded and agreed.

More light-hearted fodder followed: some hip-hop poetry about abstinence ("For me, there's no premarital lovin' because I'm stayin' pure 'til the day I'm a husbin.'") and a *funny* parody of Mastercard's priceless commercial, where a guy walks away from a date with blue balls. (One silver ring: twenty dollars. Always knowing how the night's going to end: priceless.)

Now, the serious, scared-straight-abstinence-shit was about to go down. Its message: "If you hump before marriage, all this WILL happen to you!"

Expository dialogue helped us follow a dramatic reenactment of what happens to couples after they have sex before marriage:

TOM: "Ally, wait! What has gotten into you lately? I haven't seen you at the youth group forever. And every time I see you at school, you avoid me."

ALLY: (Curtly) "I'm busy."

TOM: "Ever since you came over to my house the night my parents were gone, you've wanted nothing to do with me."

ALLY: (Curtly) "Can we please not talk about that night. It was a mistake—nothing more!"

TOM: "It can't be a mistake. (Quiet) I promised myself I was going to wait until I was married, and I threw it all away for you."

ALLY: "Every time I see you, it brings up all the guilt and shame of that night."

TOM: (Angry) "You're just as dirty as I am. You should have thought of that before you threw yourself at me. (Murmurs through crowd.)

ALLY: "I wish we had never met!"

The teens in attendance learned that premarital sex is so shameful that afterwards the other person will want nothing to do with you!

"What part of 'wait until marriage' don't they understand?" I whispered again to the somber mom next to me while wondering if there was going to be any advice on how to have healthy, fun sex once people are married.

"My name is Mackenzie. I'm going to share my story," said a girl wearing a T-shirt that read: **Don't Drink and Park. Accidents Cause Kids.** "At the end of the night, you can decide what you want your story to be."

Mackenzie had premarital, wedlock-less sex, which resulted in her becoming a homeless alcoholic trapped in an abusive relationship. How, you ask? "When I was sixteen, my boyfriend gave me an ultimatum. 'Either you sleep with me, or choose one of your friends I lose my virginity to!'"

Mackenzie ended up losing her virginity … in the school parking lot! Instead of sweet romance, all Mackenzie got was sex: "That was the only thing we would do together. It would happen again and again and again …"

The suburban Cincinnati kids absorbed Mackenzie's every word: "I found myself on my face in the bathroom of my home in the ghetto, with no heat and no running water, holding a stolen pregnancy test and pleading with the Lord that it would be negative." (See what happens!)

But the ultimate shocker came from her "boyfriend," who was also, naturally, the town drug dealer. "The entire time we were together, he'd been sleeping with my best friend!" she proclaimed. "I gave pieces of my heart away—that I can never get back. Ever!"

Eventually, Mackenzie attended a Silver Ring Thing show, and her past was forgiven—BORN-AGAIN VIRGIN-STYLE! "I put on this ring and made the commitment to wait for my future husband … and in twenty-seven days, I'll be getting married." The audience applauded this unexpected plot twist. She continued, "There's nothing you have done that prevents you from starting over tonight."

For the more maladjusted in attendance that would one day break the night's pledge, Mackenzie's story would surely help them fulfill—when they fall—a life of drug addiction and strip-club vocational undertakings.

"This commitment we talk about here tonight—it doesn't make sense to the rest of the world. We've come a long ways away from God's plan for sex," said Spence, returning to stage to close the deal. And he knew the score. Spence said he attempted suicide as a result of his premarital sexual escapades, which he claimed also left him homeless, simultaneously addicted to Oxycontin and cocaine, and spiritually lost.

Now, his hard sell: "God created sex to be between one man and one woman—in the context of marriage. It's like a wedding gift God gives you. For it to be amazing, it has to be equally as powerful. You need to use it the way I'm telling you …"

Spence, however, was forgetting that high expectations reinforce selfish desires of gratification and set up couples for crappy marriages where they will spend eternity stuck in missionary position with no hope of foreplay.

With that, the Silver Ring Thing pledge began: "If you said that prayer, then you legitimately meant it," Spence confirmed, once again adjusting his backwards baseball cap. "You're going to take that pen and fill out a commitment card."

Teens flocked to the front and filled out cards, using the backs of friends as tables. They answered questions like, "Did you pray asking God to forgive you and take control of your life?"

The abstinence pledge was similar to AA: an emergency text number was provided for moments of weakness, and Spence requested that everyone find an accountability partner (a sponsor) to check up on each other's virginity. "Ladies, your accountability partner must be a lady. Fellas, your accountability partner must be a fella."

Virginity came with a price tag: twenty dollars. "I want everyone to get a ring tonight. If you don't have the money, I want you to borrow it," Spence said, urging parents to donate money, become a ring sponsor, and stalk their kids until wedding day.

"Let's do something CRAAAAAAZY!" shouted Spence as a big, group virginity photo was snapped.

Afterwards, merchandise tables hawked all sorts of Silver Ring Thing stuff: DVDs, T-shirts, jackets, caps, stickers, and rings. The ring-purchasing reception line spilled out into the foyer. Groups of smiling kids, with outstretched ring hands, posed for more photos.

An eight-year old girl sat in the doorway, reading out loud from the Silver Ring Thing manual: "They say one day you will crack and have sex before marriage. You can't keep up this goody two-shoes act forever …" (Finally, there was a rational voice.)

"What did you guys think?" asked a neighborhood mom to a group of gawky suburban teens. "Are you glad you came?"

They weakly mumbled, "Yes," in unison.

"Later this week, do you guys want to get together and discuss what we just learned?" she asked, attempting to cement intact Christian family structures. "I'll make brownies."

A confused, shy kid—trying to look optimistic about his sexless future—piped up, "I enjoy brownies. Brownies sound awesome."

CHAPTER 11

UNBORN JESUS & THE GRIM REAPER

T**HE CALL HAD BEEN** placed. "People will be driving by, flipping you off. If you can take that sort of thing, then you're our kind of guy!" Charlie explained over the phone.

"People flip me off all the time," I enthusiastically replied. "So yeah, I can take it."

Ready to welcome a new member, Charlie informed me, "Okay, we meet Saturday mornings at 8:30 in front of the Temple of Moloch. Or as I like to call it, Planned Deathhood!"

"Can I bring my own protest signs?" I asked Charlie.

"What kind of signs do you have?" he responded, with what could have been mistaken for slight giddiness.

"I made some with poster board and markers," I replied.

"Don't worry," Charlie assured. "We have plenty of signs here!"

In retrospect, when recalling the signs, it is hard not to think of the iconic photo of Donald Trump—flanked by a group of middle-aged white men looking extremely pleased with themselves—after he had just signed an executive order to defund International Planned Parenthood and other women's health services by restoring the Mexico City Policy, which was named for a 1984 population conference where Ronald Reagan enacted a policy that prevented family planning funds from going to groups that performed abortions.

Why is it always a group of old, white men that determines what women may do with their bodies?

It was about to infiltrate this group of abortion protesters—and future Trump supporters—in order to get inside the mindset of those fanatical men who occasionally snapped and ended up shooting abortion doctors.

Using the all-American name of Monroe Peterson, I ingratiated myself with Charlie, one of the group's leaders, by telling him I was an aborted fetus who had been reincarnated for the purpose of spreading the word that abortion was wrong. I would match fanaticism with fanaticism and find out why conservatives hate Planned Parenthood so much.

Come Saturday morning, I ventured to a San Jose Planned Parenthood clinic, situated across from a YMCA in a quiet neighborhood. My fellow protesters were already in action when I arrived dressed in an elaborate outfit that had tiny baby dolls taped to my shirt and carrying a baby doll floating in a jar with the words *Stop Now!* written on the outside.

"I think I only missed one Saturday," said Charlie, who sported a mustache, stocking cap, dark sunglasses, and a video camera around his neck. A veteran of the movement, he has been picketing abortion clinics every Saturday morning for the last seventeen years.

Charlie was right: the protesters had huge signs that were a million times more elaborate than I imagined. Some of the signs, which were rigged to the back of a truck along with large American flags, looked like a blender accident gone awry.

Sheepishly, I hid my homemade, hand-lettered sign that simply stated: ***HEY-HEY! HO-HO! ABORTION HAS GOTTA GO!***

"We're just a fellowship of guys who feel it's the Lord's calling to do this. We do it for the Lord, and we do it for the babies," Charlie explained, seeming pleased to have me on board.

"Let's save two lives at a time," I said with a weak smile followed by a nervous laugh.

"I met many women who have had abortions," Charlie said. "I met one woman who's had four abortions, and I told her, 'When you get to heaven, you'll get to hold those babies.'"

I vigorously nodded my head.

Around the corner, roughly thirty-five people—on their monthly excursion from a local Catholic church—gathered on the sidewalk, singing an intense hymn. Some had brought their small kids, making it a family outing.

"It's a bit of a slow day. On Saturdays, we usually go to the Planned Parenthood in Santa Clara first," informed Dave, a soft-spoken older man in glasses and a crew-neck sweater, who was tasked with showing the Catholics the ropes while Charlie broke in the new Protestant recruits.

To appease pro-lifers, congressional Republicans, for years, have tried to eliminate the roughly three hundred million dollar federal grant program known as Title X, which funds birth control and cancer screenings at Planned Parenthood and other local family planning clinics. Less than four months into his presidency, Trump signed legislation granting states the right to withhold federal dollars from clinics that provide abortion services, even though federal law already prohibits Title X money from paying for abortions. As a result, over four million American women, the majority who live below the poverty line, stand to lose access to family planning services.

"What's the deal with the dogs?" I asked Dave, inquiring about the several stern-looking Planned Parenthood workers—adorned in Planned Parenthood smocks—who suspiciously looked on as they monitored the facility's parking lot with what seemed to be vicious German shepherds on leashes. The dogs ran and jumped around, seemingly ready for action if a protester crossed the line.

"They're there to intimidate us. One time, Curtis let his dog jump at us," Dave explained, pointing to a large Planned Parenthood employee with a gray beard. "And then he said, 'There's your dinner!' Can you imagine the mindset of that?"

I shrugged my shoulders, unable to imagine that mindset.

Meanwhile, on the sidewalk, a frowning man held up a large sign that displayed an illustrated version of a Jesus fetus with the caption: **Unborn Jesus**. Not to be confused with Kung Fu Grip Jesus or Barbie Dream House Jesus, Unborn Jesus had a full beard, which seemed like quite a feat for one still in the womb.

At the edge of the parking lot, an older Planned Parenthood worker started humming loudly, hoping that her song would disrupt the protesters' hymns. "That's Lilly," said soft-spoken Dave, shaking his head in disapproval.

He then asked why I wanted to become a sidewalk counselor. I fed Dave the exact answer he wanted to hear: "I want to save two lives at a time!"

Soft-spoken Dave looked pleased.

I wasn't done. "Also, I think it would be a great way to meet women," I added, subtly suggesting that women who have had abortions probably put out. But before Dave fully computed what I said, I quickly jumped in, correcting myself, "Yeah, that's it. I want to save two lives at a time."

Dave, who had now assumed the Mr. Miyagi role to my Karate Kid for Planned Parenthood protesting training, informed, "We can't block the driveway. When you see a car pulling into the parking lot, go up to the window and say, 'Can I give you some literature?'" He motioned toward a pamphlet that read *Simply get up and walk away* and had a God Bless America sticker affixed to the back. Dave continued, "One woman read the literature, then drove away. That's one child I've saved, and I feel pretty good about that."

Just then, a scared-looking teenage guy in a beat-up, late-model car pulled into the driveway. Soft-spoken Dave sauntered over and handed him some literature through the driver's window. Minutes later, a teenage girl slowly entered the passenger door of the beat-up car.

"The Hispanics, you'll find, are usually quite respectful," Dave said softly while walking back towards me. As the beat-up car sped away, Dave snarled, "Yeah, but he still went and had it killed."

At this point, the other protesters started to recite something in unison. Dave handed me a cross attached to some beads and asked, "Do you do the Rosary?"

I responded, "Oh, you bet I do. You bet I do, indeed!"

As I joined the two parallel lines of protesters on the sidewalk, some of them eyed me with mild speculation. Since I was clueless about the words of the Rosary, I started mouthing, "For he's a jolly good fellow," over and over again.

Soon, a microphone was passed down the line, allowing each person a chance to recite a Rosary prayer. I thought to myself, "Don't stop on me, please!" I was saved when the prayer vigil concluded with a rousing chorus of "God Bless America." I knew the words to that song and—with an added arm-swing to my presentation—piped in with fervor: "God bless America, land that I love! God bless America, my home sweet home!"

But then the focus changed. "Here comes Carl," someone yelled. Smirks and smiles followed as a man rounded the corner dressed in a grim reaper outfit! Just like that, everyone's attention shifted from Unborn Jesus to Grim Reaper Carl, the clown prince of abortion clinic protesters. Complete with skeleton mask, long black-hooded robe, sickle, and two large signs—***Death Sold Here*** and ***The Killing Place***—Carl brought levity to the group.

The thrilled kids went wild. "Mom! Mom! Can we go talk to the skeleton? Can we go talk to the skeleton?! Can we, Mom?!" screamed several kids as they ran to the Grim Reaper.

"Do a lot of people dress up in costumes at these protests?" I asked Dave.

"Sometimes," he replied.

"Is it OK if I come back in a different costume next week?" I asked Dave.

"Sure. What do you have in mind?" questioned Dave.

"Well, I have this great Ninja costume!" I said, making an excited face and a few Ninja moves.

"I one time saw an abortion-mill worker dressed in the same [Grim Reaper] costume for Halloween. Think of the mindset of that," soft-spoken Dave said, pointing to his head.

Sometimes, soft-spoken Dave was a downer.

The families from the monthly church group slowly departed, leaving behind the slightly hardened middle-aged men, much like the hardened men in the photo with Trump.

These hardcore anti-abortionists believed that women who have abortions should be punished criminally—a similar sentiment that Trump would later express on the campaign trail.

The New York Times once asked Trump—who during his bachelor days in Manhattan was an adamant believer in legal abortion—if he was "ever involved with anyone who had an abortion." Trump evasively responded, "Such an interesting question. So what's your next question?"

Like any snake oil salesman, he was playing to the emotions of the people he knew would support him: Americans who vote strictly on a candidate's position on the abortion issue. Trump was duping a cross-section of Americans, similar to Charlie and his crew, simply to gain their support.

Soon, I found myself manning a street corner next to Grim Reaper Carl. He seemed to be talking to himself.

I regrettably found myself holding a large sign that contained a graphic and disturbing full-color image accompanied by the words **The 8th Week.**

Two Planned Parenthood workers saw me in action and started to whisper in an animated fashion, clearly putting me on their crazy-list. For their benefit, I added some loud, screaming chants in the spirit of a sports fan on game day: "Two, four, six, eight! WHO DO WE APPRECIATE? JESUS! JESUS! YAY, STOP ABORTION!"

As the day progressed car after car drove by and, before flipping us off and shouting their disapprovals at what we were doing, did double-takes at the appalling blender accident signs.

"Kids can see that, you know," screamed an angry bicyclist.

"Well, what about all the kids who *can't* see it?" I retorted.

As parents picked up their children from the YMCA, I was bombarded by looks of anger from the disturbed moms and dads. But

I flashed a big, hearty smile, enthusiastically lifted high my horrific sign, and wildly gestured as if I were beckoning them to a junior high school car wash.

"Can you move your sign?" screamed a woman in an SUV, trying to depart Planned Parenthood with her teenage daughter.

"Hey! Free speech!" I yelled before bursting into another chorus of "God Bless America."

"You're blocking the view of the traffic," soft-spoken Dave explained, motioning me out of the way.

I lowered my sign and shouted at another car, "Can I give you some literature?"

To liven things, Glen, who had the demeanor of a prisoner-of-war survivor, pulled out a large, yellow boombox, cranked up the volume, and pointed it directly at the Planned Parenthood as if we were now U.S. troops blasting Metallica in order to run a Central American druglord out of his compound.

"That's something Glen likes to do. This is one of their very own tapes. It's a doctor explaining the procedure of how to give a partial abortion," Dave said with disgust. "They actually applaud at the end. Can you believe it?"

Using his own words, I repeated back to Dave, "Think of the mindset of that!"

From a passing car someone suddenly screamed, "Fuck off!" while also flipping us the finger. Glen quickly grabbed his camera and started snapping photos of the vehicle.

"I usually take a picture of anyone who flips us the bird," explained Glen while I grabbed my camera and also started snapping away. "It's for our own protection."

Soft-spoken Dave then calmly advised, "Just remember, it's against the law to take a picture of anyone going into the abortion mill."

With more than a hint of nostalgia, Dave recalled the golden age of the most radical pro-life groups: "Back in '89 I was with Operation Rescue. We used to block the doors of an abortion clinic. One time we had eight hundred people out there! A few of us ended up going to jail."

They used to employ bicycle locks along with human chains—and sometimes automobiles—to prevent people from entering abortion clinics. Now, it is a felony to block the entrance.

"You can block an animal-testing clinic," soft-spoken Dave continued. "But you can't block an abortion mill. Think about the mindset of that."

"Are you reminiscing about the good old days?" Glen piped in. We shared a hearty chuckle.

The lighthearted moment was short-lived: a police car pulled into the Planned Parenthood parking lot. Glen, once again, grabbed his camera and this time snapped a photo of the patrol car.

"That's not a good idea, Glen," advised soft-spoken Dave.

With both hands on his belt, an officer exited the squad car and gave us a "here we go, again" look. This was going to be good: direct police confrontation!

"How many times do I have to tell you, you can't have your signs on public property," the cop proclaimed, gesturing at the numerous, graphically horrific, blender-accident signs that rested against trees or were wired to street traffic poles for all the neighborhood residents to enjoy.

Glen immediately confronted the officer. "Well, how come you can hang political signs on traffic signs? We're expressing our right to freedom of speech!" he angrily retorted.

The cop remained calm as he engaged in what seemed to be a

frequent routine.

"What about that sign?" hotheaded Glen proclaimed as he pointed across the street to a YMCA construction parking sign that was posted in front of, well, the YMCA parking lot.

Soft-spoken Dave suddenly snapped, raising his voice for the first time that day, "WE DON'T WANT TO BE DISCRIMINATED AGAINST!"

Whoa! The Grim Reaper and I looked at each other in disbelief. "What's up with soft-spoken Dave, Grim Reaper!?" I proclaimed.

Glen stormed off to find reinforcements. Minutes later, he returned with a stack of papers from the Life Legal Defense Foundation and presented them to the officer.

"What are you showing me here?" asked the now annoyed officer, who shook his head in disbelief as Glen pointed to various sections of the legal papers. "This says nothing about having the right to post your signs on public property."

To no avail, I tried to help out the cause by loudly bellowing, "GOD BLESS AMERICA, LAND THAT I LOVE!"

Dave advised me to save the singing for later. The police officer agreed and then laid down the law: "You can have your signs, but you have to carry them. Do you understand?"

The officer returned to his patrol car and waited momentarily, ensuring that his commands would be followed. An uneasy feeling swept over me. Suddenly, I felt as if I were about to be struck in the back of the head by a lead pipe—wielded by either Grim Reaper Glen after he discovered that I was an abortion-protesting impostor or an angry boyfriend simply defending his newly traumatized girlfriend.

Glen invited me down for the next weekend's protests: "I usually get down here at seven in the morning."

Trying to top his fanaticism, I replied, "Oh, yeah? Well, *I'll* be down here at six-thirty."

Now ready to leave, I grabbed my jar with the aborted baby doll floating in water. It accidentally slipped between my fingers and fell to the ground, smashing into pieces and freeing the doll. As I looked at Glen, Charlie, soft-spoken Dave, and the Grim Reaper, my eyes welled up with tears.

I wouldn't be back the next weekend, but I left knowing that this group of men would continue to incite fear by telling women what to do with their bodies. I showed up masquerading as an extremist in order to understand the mindset of extremists. But I departed just as scared as I was when I arrived. It was now up to these zealots—without me—to "save" two lives at a time.

CHAPTER 12

HIT ME WITH YOUR BEST EX-GAY SHOT

THE LEADER OF THE support group I infiltrated pulled me aside and announced, "Okay, time to get into the hot seat!" I was herded to the center of a small room where I sat down and bowed my head.

Suddenly, twelve Fellow Warriors—or "ex-gays," as their propaganda calls them—put their hands on my body, most particularly the shoulders and upper torso, and the praying began. Like a group of freestyle rappers, each took a turn putting hands on me and praying that my sinful soul stayed away from the world of, as Donald Trump would put it, "The Gays."

"Monty has a scary journey ahead ..."

"Evil days! Evil days!"

"... please watch over Monty, oh Lord!"

"Amen! Amen!"

"The righteous man falls several times. Look after and guide Monty!"

"Yes, Jesus! Yes!"

I was going by the pseudonym Monty, and the Fellow Warriors were praying that the Lord would prevent me from falling back into "the gay lifestyle." But this laying of hands exceeded my comfort zone. When the praying finally stopped, someone handed me a box of Kleenex. Apparently, they expected me to be in tears.

"Wow!" I remarked, moving my hands to emulate some sort of energy field. "Yeah, it felt like a force or something like that. Yeah, that's it: a force!"

I paused, not knowing what else to say. As the twelve Fellow Warriors kept staring at me, I once again exclaimed, "Wow!"

I was undercover in the weird gay-hating world of conversion therapy, which conservative Christian ministries believe can change a person's sexual orientation.

Some might think that only fringe cult members back this pseudoscience, right? Wrong! U.S. Vice President Mike Pence, who has a long history of using anti-gay rhetoric, believes in providing federal dollars to "those seeking to change their sexual behavior." And his boss, Donald J. Trump, has banned transgender individuals from serving in the military.

Add that to the ambitions of homophobe Jeff Sessions, Trump's former Attorney General, who filed arguments with the Supreme Court in support of a Colorado bakery that was sued because its owner refused to make a cake for a gay wedding, and the rights of the LGBTQIA community stand to suffer.

With this complicit support of current administration officials, it's not surprising that muckraking religious groups, like the Family Research Council, still exist while firmly professing the pseudo-science of conversion therapy, which they now have rebranded as Sexual Attraction Fluidity Exploration in Therapy—or "SAFE-T" for short.

Family Research Council President and anti-gay zealot Tony Perkins has gone as far as equating homosexuality with pedophilia. According to the group's website:

> *Homosexual conduct is harmful to the persons who engage in it and to society at large, and can never be affirmed. It is by definition unnatural, and as such is associated with negative physical and psychological health effects. While the origins of same-sex attractions may be complex, there is no convincing evidence that a homosexual identity is ever something genetic or inborn ... Sympathy must be extended to those who struggle with unwanted same-sex attractions, and every effort should be made to assist such persons to overcome those attractions, as many already have.*

Despite psychological evidence debunking conversion therapy, groups like the Family Research Council believe that homosexuality is something that can be treated and cured—like poison ivy or frostbite—by embracing Jesus Christ.

In 2014 the UN Committee Against Torture (CAT) heard testimony from the National Center for Lesbian Rights (NCLR) officials, who lobbied the United Nations in an effort to adopt legislation that would ban attempts to change a minor's sexual orientation or gender identity via conversion therapy.

CAT heard from NCLR's Samantha Ames and an ex-gay therapy survivor, Samuel Brinton. The two traveled to Geneva as part of their organization's #BornPerfect campaign, whose purpose is to end the practice of attempting to change a person's sexual orientation, which it equates to torture and child abuse. NCLR has already worked to ban conversion therapy for minors in California and New Jersey. Legislation is also being considered in New York, Massachusetts, and Illinois.

Meanwhile, these conservative Christian groups continue to dish out their psychologically damaging methodology to vulnerable people overcome by religious guilt. In order to understand their manifesto, which advocates that homosexuality can be cured by embracing an attractive man with long hair and washboard-abs (Jesus), I journeyed into the world of conversion therapy by posing as a confused gay man in need of guidance. If the Fellow Warriors couldn't "cure" me, I was headed straight to hell.

I first found myself in Sacramento, sitting inside a small office at a church community center, ready for some conversion therapy. Several pictures of Jesus hung on the wall, along with a framed portrait that read: *Can Homosexuality Be Cured? The Answer is YES!* I was handed a pamphlet—portraying smiling, well-groomed men hugging smiling, well-groomed women—with the following verbiage:

Proclaiming Victory Over HOMOSEXUALITY
How Should the Church Respond?

- *Do not fear the homosexuals.*
- *Recognize that at the core of the homosexual struggle, there is a deep-seated sense of rejection.*
- *Ask the Lord to open a door of communication.*
- *Pray for them.*

"The best relationship you'll ever have is with Jesus Christ," explained a large man named Curtis, dishing out a Christian cliché. After struggling with homosexual temptations in college, he claimed to be "cured."

We sat across from each other, and Curtis asked me—playing a confused gay man—to describe my history of same-sex attractions. When trying to drive home a point with a personal anecdote, he several times referred to himself in the third person. As I tried to find loopholes in his logic, Curtis developed an eye tic that apparently required rapid blinking.

"I used to look into what is best for the church of Curtis," he said.

Curtis, who cast away the homosexual devil and is now married to a woman, listened intensely as we sat alone in his office and I slowly rubbed my chest while going into graphic sexual details about my sordid (and fictitious) past, which involved a hedonistic month-long tea-bagging binge.

"If you let Jesus into your life, then he will go right to the trouble area and help you with whatever you are struggling with," advised Curtis, who prescribed—like methadone for heroin addicts—the Christ-cure for all sins.

"So, Jesus is just like a personal trainer?" I asked.

Curtis smiled: "I like that."

I offered, "Feel free to use that if you want."

Curtis informed me of the many perks of becoming an ex-gay, which included a lifetime of complete and utter celibacy. He then again reached for his oft-used catchphrase: "The best relationship you'll ever have is with Jesus Christ!"

There was no mindfuck here: just shaky and discredited science. Like the Silver Ring Thing Christians, these religious zealots relied on the Bible as their main medical science journal.

In 2009 the American Psychological Association condemned conversion therapy: "Mental health professionals should avoid telling clients that they can change their sexual orientation through therapy or other treatments." Four years later, Exodus International, an organization whose mission was to "help" gay Christians become straight, shut down after thirty-seven years and issued an apology to the gay community for "years of undue judgment by the organization and the Christian Church as a whole."

As far as homoerotic imagery goes, a barely clothed Jesus on the cross is pretty high up there on the list. On the other hand, anti-gay Christian groups fail to see the irony when claiming that the main reason men fall into the "gay lifestyle" is because they don't have a personal relationship with Jesus (i.e., these groups don't want men to be gay, but the only way not to be gay is to have a personal relationship with a man). It was time to seek more unqualified ex-gay treatment. I called a number listed on a Christian website.

"Are you professional counselors?" I asked a man named José, who was assigned to help me through my ordeal.

To my surprise, José openly acknowledged his lack of credentials: "No, we are not professional counselors. We're people who have dealt with same-sex attractions ourselves. Or we are people who have a desire to help people that do."

José explained the cure: "Recovery is not something that happens overnight. Yes, there have been people who have said yes, it's happened for them overnight. Some people think if the sexual side of things is gone, then they are cured more or less. We call it the process, because it is a process of recovery."

I then referenced an ex-gay website, which said that male homosexuality can start as a result of envy of the size of someone else's Johnson, and asked, "Do you think it's like envy?"

José replied, "You know, just from reading up, I think it could be envy of other guys, like if they are more well-endowed ... that could be an envy trait."

I told José that for me, it was the complete opposite: "I was much larger than all the other kids in that department."

"Uh-huh," answered José before quickly changing the subject. "Heterosexuality is not our overall goal, because we have a lot of married people come to us. Our main goal is to help them with their relationship with Christ, and from there, sexuality will change them into the person that God created us to be."

Now it was time to turn the religious tables. Since these conversion therapy groups stressed that people fall into the gay lifestyle because they lack Jesus in their lives, what if Jesus were the source of the problem?

"It's kind of weirdly religious-based for me," I said.

"Uh-huh," José responded.

"It's kind of a messed-up sort of scenario. It's really complicated," I told him.

"There's actually different roots and different causes," José said. "Some people stem from a sense of envy. Some stem from a sense of anger and rejection. It would really depend on each individual person."

While wondering if he was reading from a telemarketing script, I asked, "Has this case ever come up? The first time I ever felt attracted to a man—this sounds kind of weird—when I was little, I would have this picture of Jesus hanging in my room, and at night it would get me aroused. I mean really, really aroused."

There was a long silence before I continued.

"Now, I try to go to church and get close to Jesus, but these sexual feelings come up, and it's really inappropriate," I told him. "I only end up getting REALLY turned on ... you know ... fully erect!"

After long pause, José finally responded, "Okay."

I was directed to a Christ-centered ministry designed to help men struggling with homosexuality leave their past lifestyle and fully "EMBRACE THEIR TRUE IDENTITY IN JESUS CHRIST."

If a group ever were to organize a gay-shame parade, this group would have been it. The ex-gay support group's monthly Friday night meeting was held in Marin County, north of San Francisco, at a generic two-story office complex. About a dozen ex-gays were gathered in a circle as I entered a cramped back office filled with numerous books on the subject at hand.

"Welcome Monty and Steven," announced the second-in-command with excited eyes. He was wearing an oversized wooden cross around his neck as if he were the Flavor Flav of Christianity. "It's their first night. Make them feel welcome."

After being trumpeted as fresh meat, I took my lead from the other new guy, Steven, a teenager with tattoos on his knuckles, who tightly gripped a Bible while staring straight ahead with the crazed look of a serial killer about ready to snap.

For the most part, it was a congenial bunch. I was offered tea and cookies. Only two really old guys could be described as "creepy." (They remained silent throughout the meeting.) I was instructed to take my place on the cozy couch next to the second-in-command. As laughter and talk of a "fallen member" who was back in the lifestyle died down, the meeting began.

"Father, thank you for turning my life around," prayed the leader, who mildly resembled Mel Gibson with thirty years of hard living under his belt. Like a wise ex-gay prophet, he explained how the "program" began in 1995, bitterly noting, "That's when I started my walk out of this mess."

The group's goal wasn't necessarily for members to turn heterosexual but for them to become holy in God's eyes. Okay, if the group knew that its members couldn't just turn straight, I wondered how it felt about the transgender bathroom issue.

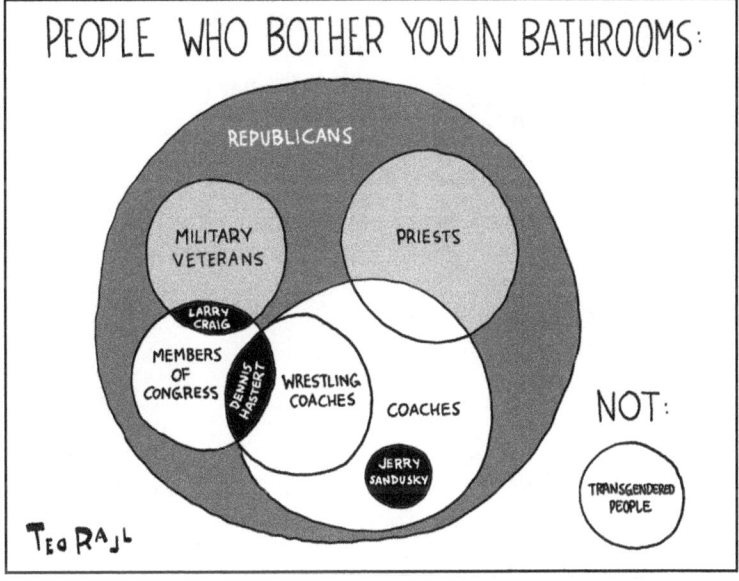

"The focus right now is walking with the Lord," said the leader. "When it's time, God will pray my wife into me."

He told the group how hard it was to deal with same-sex attraction. "Several years ago, there was some construction going on down there. And there was this kid down there. Really nice body," he said. "And he would have the jackhammer going and have his shirt off."

Laughter erupted, and I sensed that some "ex-gays" were getting slightly aroused.

"It's important to recognize that men are attracted to men. We're drawn to masculinity. There's nothing sexual about it," explained the leader, which prompted me to wonder where guys who are into Thai lady-boys fit into this definition.

As the conversation devolved into a discussion about masturbation—who was doing it, when, and why—it became clear—surprisingly, or perhaps not so—that almost all of the group members were dealing with serious drug and alcohol abuse issues. Yet they attributed their most severe problems to being caught up in the gay lifestyle.

"I lost my job, my house, everything."

"I did a lot of coke."

"I got to go to my twelve-step meeting tomorrow."

"My sexual drive was not normal."

"When I was in the deepest, darkest depths of my sin, that's when Christ died for me."

The group members believed that personal excess and general life screw-ups, which were probably symptoms of underlying psychological issues that arose from denying their true sexualities, resulted from simply being gay.

The leader, who did not have a psychological degree, explained that homosexuality has nothing to do with sex. "It's not a sexual problem. It's a relationship problem. Men feed off of each other's masculinity," he said, stressing each word. "It's a relationship problem!"

"Exactly."

"Repent."

"Uh-huh."

"And that's the key. God, he accepts me with all my frailty in all my screwed-up-ness," the leader continued. "But he has the plan, the desire, to transform me into something that is going to bring him glory."

"Exactly."

"Repent."

"Uh-huh."

"When I had a wife, I was not intimate. When I had a lover, I was not intimate," a guy in a baseball cap added. "God was showing me that it was lust, because you don't know the difference."

Then, the second-in-command asked, "What about Monty and

Steven? Do you want to share anything?"

By this point, I had forgotten that I was calling myself Monty and was momentarily caught off guard.

Since everyone there had a drug or alcohol problem and had slept with thousands of partners, I needed to switch up my game plan. How would they counsel someone who was quite normal but just happened to be gay? So, I told the group that I had never touched drugs or alcohol and that I had been in one long, monogamous relationship with the same guy.

"CANNIBALISM!" the group shouted in near-unison.

The leader explained cannibalism, again slowly stressing one word at a time: "You-take-on-the-attributes-of-the-other-person."

While turning to me and nodding, the second-in-command said, "I know. I was in a relationship for seventeen years."

In summing up my situation and all other gay scenarios, the leader added, "Men want lust, not intimacy."

A guy across the circle leaned toward me with strong, crazed eye contact. Then, he gave it to me straight: "An erection put into a woman's vagina is like going into the paradise of heaven. An erection put in anything else is unnatural, and it's a sin!"

Politely smiling and nodding, I replied, "Okay."

While keeping eye contact with vagina man, he began to make elaborate hand gestures and then proceeded to utilize the word "erection" six more times. When he stopped directing the word "erection" at me, I felt very grateful.

"Can I still hang around my old friends?" I asked. "We've all got the same taste in music."

Steven—still tightly gripping his Bible—suddenly sat up and for the first time that evening piped in, "I'll answer that. An alcoholic shouldn't go into a bar!"

And the leader stressed, "It will be worth the sacrifice. You'll find the best relationship you'll ever have will be with God."

I felt bad for these guys. Clearly, they were confusing drug and alcohol problems, coupled with sex addiction and extreme guilt, with supposed sins against their God and the world.

Their heartfelt comments were nothing if not depressing:

To become a heterosexual is not my goal; my goal is holiness, spirituality.

Images still plague my mind, but I dismiss them at the door.

I used to think that Jesus loves drag queens. Now, I know it's wrong.

This all sounded so sad and very lonely, with the only two options provided by their religion: heterosexuality or celibacy. Yet these men, obviously, weren't into women—and never would be.

"I work around a lot of homosexuals, so what should I do?" I asked the leader, who had absolutely no professional counseling accreditations.

"You might consider changing jobs," he strongly advised.

"But I work as a costume designer for musical theater," I said. "That's what I do. I can't really change jobs. That's how I make a living."

The leader suggested putting up a barrier "because they will try to tempt you."

"Amen!"

"Exactly!"

I questioned the leader: "First you're saying to develop nonsexual relationships with men. Then, you're saying to put up a wall?"

The leader had an easy solution: "Just say, 'Hey, I'm a Christian now!'" To illustrate his point, he raised his hand in a "stop" gesture.

"I used to be a DJ at a top gay nightclub in New York," said the former coke enthusiast in the baseball cap. "It's worth the sacrifice. Give yourself to God."

Now came the part of the meeting where the Fellow Warriors made me sit in the "hot seat." As the ex-gays put their hands on and prayed over me, I swore that one of them was massaging my shoulder.

"Evil days! Evil days!"

"Amen! Amen!"

Afterward, the guy wearing a large, wooden homemade cross pulled me aside. I was worried that he might be calling my bluff. Instead, he said, "The Lord showed me a sadness in you."

He had my number.

DON'T TAKE AWAY OUR GUNS

PART FOUR

INTRODUCTION
ARMED TO THE TEETH

A MERICAN EXCEPTIONALISM IS THE belief that the United States is different (better) than other nations. China may have better high-speed rail and England may have superior healthcare, but the U.S. stands head and shoulders above all other nations. This belief is repeatedly expressed and expounded upon by corporate heads and their chief propagandists, school teachers, journalists and editorial writers, and politicians.

Ronald Reagan (by way of the Puritan authoritarian John Winthrop) called America "a shining city on a hill." During the campaign, Hillary Clinton (via Tocqueville) said, "We are great because we are good." Michelle Obama: "This right now is the greatest country on Earth."

It's safe to say, for the most part, that the majority of Americans believe it. There's something special about the U.S. in a way that there isn't something particularly unique about, say, Portugal or Mauritius.

That's what Americans like to think, anyway.

If there's anything great about our increasingly frequent mass shootings—and granted, you have to work hard to find a silver lining to a pile of bodies riddled with AR-15 bullets in a church, a school cafeteria, or at a country-music festival—is the fact that it's a form of exceptionalism that doesn't cast the U.S. in the most flattering light.

Try as you might, you can't find another country where crazy white guys routinely freak out and kill a bunch of people for not much reason at all—or perhaps no reason whatsoever, other than they can because buying a really big military-grade gun is easy and relatively cheap. Mass shootings, and the gun culture that spawn them, are a uniquely American phenomenon. And like the crazy Trump fanatics and the Christian conservatives the liberal pundits of the West and East Coasts managed to ignore before 2016, the Gun Thing is a very real, very big, and really widespread Thing.

It kind of takes the winds out of the sails of any suggestion that the U.S. has anything to teach Portugal or Mauritius.

You may have heard of "mansplaining," which is when a dude patronizingly explains something to a woman, often concerning a subject about which she knows more than he does (c.f., rape culture, workplace discrimination, etc.). Other spin-off portmanteaus mocking pompous people of privilege include whitesplaining (white person explains racism to black person), straightsplaining, Millennialsplaining, and even gunsplaining.

May the victory of Donald Trump mark the long overdue death of Ameri-splaining—when American leaders like Clinton and Obama (and not a few ordinary citizens) pretentiously declaim our nation's supposed exceptionalism to people in countries that do a better job than we do.

First and foremost, I'd like to thank Trump for his campaign slogan: ***Make America Great Again.*** Granted, he wasn't talking to blacks and other oppressed segments of society for whom the past is more about pain than nostalgia. Trump's campaign was aimed at whites. Nevertheless, Trump deserves credit for acknowledging that—at least at this time—America is not so great. He calls us "a Third World country." Keep reading, and you'll see that he has a point.

The first step is acknowledging that you have a problem.

Problems? Where to start?

Our economic structure sucks. We're the world's richest nation. But because we also have the most horrendous wealth inequality, most Americans are poor. According to the UN, our poverty rate is worse than seventeen of the nineteen OECD countries. We have the highest rate of childhood poverty. But the rich pigs in charge don't care, which is why we have the worst social safety net.

Maybe before Ameri-splaining human rights to Iran, where free RouhaniCare for everyone (!) rolled out in 2018, we should stop letting people die of cancer because they're poor. Similarly, before telling the Iranians they're wrong to execute children, we might want to stop doing the same thing.

Our infrastructure is outdated and poorly maintained. It would take an additional three trillion six hundred billion dollars to bring our existing highways, bridges, dams, sewers, water pipes, rail, and so on up to code—yet spending on repairs is at a thirty-year low. That doesn't count the five hundred billion dollars or more it would cost to build a high-speed rail system like they have in Europe and Japan— you know, modern countries.

Rather than harassing China over their ridiculous little fake islands, perhaps U.S. officials could invite the brilliant civil engineers creating a high-speed train system—complete with pressurization like a plane as it soars through and around some of the biggest mountains on the planet—to Tibet to show us how to bring our trains into the twenty-first century.

What is with us? Why do we talk down to the rest of the world from the depths of the lowest swamp, well below the moral high ground? During his penultimate State of the Union address, President Obama Ameri-splained to Russia's Vladimir Putin his "aggressive" annexation of Crimea. At the time, the U.S. was in its fourteenth year of occupying Afghanistan, its twelfth of occupying Iraq, and was bombing the crap out of Yemen, where Obama's death drones were killing thousands of people, most of whom he thought were innocent.

When you stop to imagine what we look like to the rest of the world, we're lucky that, thus far, we got away with just one wee 9/11.

Will Ameri-splaining continue under Trump? You'd think not, but since he's already swiveled one hundred eighty degrees on so many other issues, he easily could revert from his current, refreshing pessimism to Bush-Obama-style triumphalism. The difference now is, no one—not even here in America where no one reads anything— can possibly take the U.S. government seriously when it scolds some country for, say, torturing people. Whereas Obama condescendingly told his successor that torture doesn't work (but not that it's immoral—or that he still allowed the CIA to use it), Trump has said of waterboarding, "I like it a lot."

The United States has always been corrupt, savage, and brutal. It has always been wildly dysfunctional and hypocritical. But now, thanks to a president who is loudly ignorant and utterly devoid of impulse control, the mask is off. The horrible truth about the United States can no longer be denied.

Trump epitomizes truth in advertising. We're a nasty, crappy country.

President Trump suits us fine.

The trouble is, his followers are not that bright—yet they're armed to the teeth.

–**Ted Rall**

Come along with **Harmon** into gun country as he infiltrates some Trump followers who are armed to the teeth ...

CHAPTER 13

NOT ON OUR WATCH

A**S THE SOUND OF** gunfire rumbled in the distance, the tense and paranoid backroom of Westside Pistol Range was like an Alex Jones Infowars discussion board come to life. Amalia, a union carpenter, arrived late and had a lot on her mind. "If everything were to collapse, we'd still be working, but without any kind of compensation," she stated with certainty while shuffling through a handful of notes from her independent research. "They could just take us—because they kind of own us!"

The group listened intently to her words. Before she arrived, we went around the circle and non-ironically read the Constitution, which fired up everyone.

"When the banks fail they can confiscate our assets and not pay us back," said the large man seated behind me as gunshots accented his words.

"I'll probably get food and shelter in a FEMA camp. That's my compensation," added a concerned Amalia.

"I believe what she's talking about is a military manual from the last couple of years that was released on Civilian Management," said Rick.

Resentful of an America that they believed was spinning out of control, the fifteen people present that day wanted to take charge of their own lives and hold onto their guns. So, these patriots had armed themselves to the teeth in order to stand against what they considered "unconstitutional" orders from an increasingly tyrannical government.

"They create a 'false flag'—like registering the ammunition," said Joe, a blue-collar worker from the Queens, who was full of conspiracy theories. "So you create the fear in the people. They go nuts and buy everything up. And now you know who owns what—without coming forward and saying, 'You're going to have to register your gun.'

"The government then has a record of these sales that they can track through credit cards and online. They control the Internet!"

I nodded my head in firm agreement with the other members of the group. Welcome to the world of the Oath Keepers, a far-right vigilante organization whose nightmare anti-Utopian vision of *Amerika* has citizens rounded up by their own government and placed in giant concentration camps. To an Oath Keeper, everything is a conspiracy.

The Oath Keepers claim to be a non-partisan, libertarian-leaning organization largely comprised of active duty and retired police officers, firefighters, and military. Founded in 2009 by Yale-educated attorney, former army paratrooper, and Ron Paul staffer Stewart Rhodes, the group sees itself as the "Guardians of the Republic," and its mission is "to defend the Constitution against all enemies, foreign and domestic."

Since 2005, when hurricane Katrina devastated New Orleans, the Oath Keepers have feared that martial law will be instigated during a future disaster and every American placed in a 24-7 government-run FEMA camp. To help prevent this overreach, the group lives by its clever motto: **NOT ON OUR WATCH.**

But the group is more than just a motto. The Oath Keepers swear to fight back against overly militarized police departments and unconstitutional acts by the government.

During the riots that followed the shooting death of Michael Brown, who was killed by a white police officer, armed Oath Keepers mysteriously appeared on Ferguson, Missouri rooftops with the stated mission of securing local businesses. However, when the St.

Louis County police emerged from the shattered glass of ransacked buildings, the vigilante group was ordered to leave the rooftops or be arrested for operating security without a license, which only added fuel to their conspiracy that the government does not protect its people.

Oath Keepers headed to the Nevada desert in 2014 to assist rancher Cliven Bundy during his armed stand-off against Federal Bureau of Land Management agents. Critics were alarmed at the government's decision to withdraw in the face of armed resistance, claiming that it set a dangerous precedent and emboldened militia groups such as the Oath Keepers, whose raison d'être is trumpeted on their website:

- *We will NOT obey any order to disarm the American people.*
- *We will NOT obey any order to force American citizens into any form of detention camps under any pretext.*
- *We will NOT obey orders to assist or support the use of any foreign troops on U.S. soil against the American people to "keep the peace" or to "maintain control" during any emergency, or under any other pretext. We will consider such use of foreign troops against our people to be an invasion and an act of war.*

Sounds frightening, right? For forty dollars per year anyone can become a member of the Oath Keepers and be invited to attend their monthly meetings. Many people on the left, center, and right agree with some of the group's legitimate concerns: the government is too big, the twenty trillion dollar deficit is too large, and the growing militarization of the police is dangerous to democracy.

But, for most people, is that where a similar ideology ends? Could these misunderstood patriots—militia survivalists barking at the moon about an elite cabal that supposedly controls the world—be the true saviors of the Republic? Or were they part of a pending great anti-liberal, right-led counterrevolution that wants to shoot lefties and take names?

I wanted to know what was preventing the Oath Keepers from becoming a mainstream political force. With an extra forty bucks in my pocket, I set out to have these questions answered by becoming an official member of the Oath Keepers.

Dressed in army camouflage, I walked down a long hallway inside the Westside Pistol Range, following the sound of gunfire. A man behind a display of pistols directed me to the backroom of the gun range. Nervous, sweaty, and apprehensive, I was ready to come face-to-face with the Oath Keepers.

"Is this where the Oath Keeper meeting is?" I said to the other early-arrivers, who eyed me with suspicion. I entered the room, which was filled mostly with hardworking blue-collar guys—middle-aged men sporting mustaches and wearing plaid. Also in attendance were two women who looked like Marge Simpson's sisters, Patty and Selma, and another new member who looked slightly out of place.

I took my spot under a big *Don't Tread on Me* flag and tightly clutched a copy of the Constitution, hoping that my new peers would embrace my presence. It felt as though all the oxygen had been drained from the room.

"How did you hear about the Oath Keepers?" asked the large man situated at the front of the room near a poster that said: *This Is Not Your Daddy's .45*.

"I'm a member," I replied while whipping out my membership card—in my alias Hank Leonard—and giving my best *I belong here* look.

When Bill—the local Oath Keeper leader (and long-bearded 1950s folk singer look-alike)—arrived, the tone shifted from tense to serious. "This giant behemoth [U.S. Government]—it's not just overrun the states; it's overrunning the world," explained Bill. "This economic system—this New World Order—the only thing we can do is get back to small groups like this."

Bill referred to our small group as the regional Oath Keepers Alpha Team, which made me a part of the local elite. "Do we have new ham operators in the group?" he then asked. "How many ham operators in this room now?"

Many hands went up, including a few members with portable ham radios attached to their belts—in case the shit went down at the meeting and they needed to communicate off the grid.

"I have a couple of hand-helds and a base station," answered a man wearing an Oath Keepers T-shirt. "It's the 8 57B."

Then, Rick entered. Other members shouted his name as if he were the Oath Keepers' version of Norm from *Cheers*.

Finally, it was time to get down to business. "Does everyone have a copy of the Constitution?" asked Jack, the second in command. "Who needs one?"

Surprisingly, everyone had a copy.

"Do you have a copy," he asked me.

"Yes," I said. "Right here."

My personal pocket Constitution was mailed to me when I paid the forty dollar Oath Keeper membership fee. I passed up the one thousand dollar lifetime membership, payable in fifty dollar monthly installments. Along with my personal pocket Constitution, I received Oath Keeper bumper stickers, business cards, brochures, and my laminated membership card with matching certificate. All items were emblazoned with **NOT ON OUR WATCH**. Estimated cost of entire Oath Keepers membership pack (including shipping): two bucks.

"Someone suggested we discuss the executive actions," Bill said as a rapid series of gunfire blasted in the background. So, we read the Constitution. As we went around the circle, each Oath Keeper—in a thick New York accent—took a turn reading a passage: "The executive Power shall be vested in a President of the United States of America …"

Here we were, just a bunch of Americans reading the Constitution in the backroom of a gun range—nothing weird here. Much like group Bible study, where believers similarly interpret an old document in a way that suits their agenda, reading the Constitution was fun.

"Thanks for coming. Welcome to the family!" said Jack.

"Yeah, this was really fun," sarcastically said the other new member as she abruptly departed, leaving behind her complimentary copy of the Constitution on her desk.

As she fled the meeting room, the gun-grab quackery didn't miss a beat. "No one will ever be able to buy an AR-15 in New York State again. Ever!" claimed Bill with a hint of sadness. "They're slowly going to disarm the population."

One of the Simpson sisters, Janet, was ready to change the topic and delve into some really batshit crazy conspiracy lunacy. "It's getting so crazy out there," she said. "They're saying there are actual actors who are playing parts in these false flag events."

Another Oath Keeper confirmed this theory, which was made popular by bloated nutjob Alex Jones. "Yeah, crisis actors," he called them. The crowd rumbled.

The theory goes like this: at mass shooting tragedies, such as Sandy Hook, professional actors are hired to portray grieving family members on TV newscasts. Conspiracists see these horrific events as merely "false flags" that were orchestrated by the government in order to grab up firearms from our nation's gun owners.

"Gabby Gifford is one of those actors," Jack claimed, referring to the former Arizona Congresswoman who was severely wounded when a gunman shot her through the head at point blank range during a rally. After recovering from her injuries, she returned to public service and became an outspoken advocate for gun control. But the Oath Keepers don't believe the "official story." For them, the shooting—in which the gunman also killed six people and wounded thirteen others—was a complete lie.

"If you look on the Internet under Gabby Gifford, she is found out to be another actor with a whole different identity," Jack said.

A conspiracy of this magnitude would have required large numbers of people keeping silent about their involvement in the ruse, which would be unfeasible in the technological age, where social media posts display smartphone videos of frat guys chanting the n-word. (But what if that video was planted by the government to distract us from an upcoming federal gun-grab?!)

Sweat formed on Rick's brow as he offered an explanation. "You get a lot of people yammering over here about something bad that goes down—Sandy Hook—or whatever," he said. "So you got this conflict right? That's what it's about —always having conflict in the world.

"And then what happens? Liberals are going to step in and do the right thing for the little kids ... so that gives a platform for the government to come in and do what? TAKE MORE CONTROL! We're so caught up in guns, in gay marriage, in social issues ... in BULLSHIT that doesn't even affect OUR lives!"

True—unless you are a gay person who was denied the right of marriage ... or a congresswoman who was shot in the face at point blank while people on the Internet buzzed that you were simply "an actor" faking it. But that's off topic.

To devotees of this worldview, shooting tragedies are hoaxes perpetrated by the government in an attempt to disarm its citizens and force them into FEMA camps. Apparently, these nefarious baby-eaters have such disregard for humanity—especially gun owners—that they spend billions of dollars staging so-called "mass shootings" instead of enacting simple gun control legislation.

"With all this staging and false flags," piped in the other Simpson sister, "we're trying to work with the government and fight sovereignty ... but who are we really fighting? There's something big there!"

With an extreme poker face, I mumbled, "Not on our watch!"

Conspiracies don't drive a legitimate political force. It was just arrogant, paranoid asshole-ery at its highest form. But maybe there was more to the Oath Keepers than thin theories of cabal trickery?

No, just more talk of the Illuminati. "Honestly, I don't see independent voting as the answer," concluded Janet, "if the Vatican runs both parties."

Then, someone started a discussion about how we are all chained to the same powers in the Washington swamp.

"The problem is you got every congressperson, every judge in the back pocket of the powers that be," Janet continued. "What justice are you going to get?"

The discussion quickly devolved into more false flag and anti-Muslim rants as the Oath Keepers talked over each other in a cacophony of voices riddled with the echoing gunfire. It must be exhausting to view the world through this paranoid filter.

With nothing better to do, I mentally retreated from the group and began to ponder the meaning of a gun poster on the wall that proclaimed: *Forget 911. I Dial .357.*

"Have we heard from anybody that hasn't spoken up yet?" Jack said, directing his attention at me and interrupting my daydream.

"I'm just taking it all in," I answered truthfully.

Bill then posed a solution to combat an evil government that rigs elections, controls the media, and hires actors to stage false flags. "You got to go with the small grassroots groups," he said. "I've been involved with a lot of groups that have been coming from the same sort of inspiration as the Oath Keepers when it comes to guns and shooting."

Rick agreed: "Maybe we could open people's eyes to the fact that certain things are blown out of proportion—like arguments about race. These are all put out there to keep us separated." That's an easy thing for a privileged white guy to brush off.

"Before I found this group, I was on the couch listening to Alex Jones for years," chimed in Kevin about his main source for news. He then proposed a call to action that he had devised with the New Jersey Oath Keepers. "We're going to erect billboards near Fort Dix—for inbound/outbound traffic. That's what I offer to you …"

Janet, perplexed by the enormity of the Matrix, was clearly frustrated. "I'm looking at how big this thing is. The President's power is to the point where he has the powers of a king. The Civil War never ended," she ranted. "How is building a billboard going to help?"

Anger, discontentment, and a mutual feeling of abandonment circled the backroom of the gun range as steady gunfire continued to erupt in the background. If only someone would come along and go to Washington D.C. to "drain the swamp" Janet was talking about.

The tension built until Janet crossed an Oath Keeper line: "The Constitution could really be interpreted in so many different ways …"

Rick snapped: "No it can't! THERE'S ONLY ONE WAY!"

Much like the other fringe group meetings I had attended, this gathering turned into something that resembled an anti-government AA meeting: talk of the New World Order, the Anunnaki reptilian race, mandatory adult vaccines, implanted RFID chips, NSA monitoring through Barbie dolls, and the Bilderberg Group.

"I got to put a billboard," said an Oath Keeper who escaped Soviet Russia as a teenager. "Even if no tangible results come of it … I feel better. It's like I get this oxygen that I need so I can breathe. So if we put a billboard, that's going to be pure oxygen."

Blue-collar Joe added: "My biggest concerns are my wife and two daughters. I don't see how to make any significant change in the next one, two, three election cycles."

Finally, it was Rick's turn to put everything into perspective. "We're not going to be able to undo what has already been done," he said, "and it's going to take a while. I know I'm going to my grave, and it won't be resolved." After a long pause, Rick added, "If groups like the Oath Keepers do anything, it's waking people up."

I looked around the room one last time at Kevin, Rick, Jack, Bill, and the rest of the Alpha Team: hardworking Americans who soon became prime targets of Trump's *Make America Great Again* propaganda. When I encountered these Oath Keepers, they were just a group of angry, sad, confused, and frustrated citizens who vented their frustrations by meeting in the back of a shooting range surrounded by the steady pop of gunfire.

These lost souls—not knowing where to turn and attributing their shortcomings to a system that they believe is rigged against them—clutched their ham radios and screamed at the midday sun, uttering: left wing, right wing—just opposite wings of the same ugly bird.

Not on our watch.

CHAPTER 14
JANIE GOT A GUN ... ON FACEBOOK

THE MAYBE SOCIETY

D**ONALD TRUMP SAYS HE'S** packing heat. "I always carry a weapon on me," he claimed in 2016. "If I'd been at the Bataclan [concert mass shooting perpetrated by ISIS in Paris] or one of those bars, I would have opened fire. Perhaps I would have died, but at least I would have taken a shot. The worst thing is the powerlessness to respond to those who want to kill you."

As *The New York Times* reported in October 2017, "Nothing Divides Voters Like Owning a Gun." According to SurveyMonkey data, in the 2016 election "gun-owning households (roughly a third in America) backed Mr. Trump by 63 percent to 31 percent, while households without guns backed Mrs. Clinton, 65 percent to 30 percent."

Then there's the ease of purchase issue. From Columbine to Sandy Hook to Las Vegas, mass shootings with semiautomatic weapons often prompt people to ask, "Why is it so easy to for anyone to get ahold of military-grade weapons?" I blundered into part of the answer.

The idea came to me while sitting on the subway in New York City, where like any typical commuter I was browsing through a copy of *Tactical Weapons*. I'd just left the magazine's editorial offices after interviewing for a job to become a member of the magazine's web team. The editor contacted me out of the blue, which struck me as amusing, after seeing my résumé on MediaBistro. *Tactical Weapons* magazine had done a less thorough background check on me than an average gun dealer would (maybe) do on a mentally unstable person trying to buy an AK-47.

My interview seemed to go well, despite the fact that I was suited up for action like Robert De Niro in *Taxi Driver*, complete with stocking cap, patterned shirt, solid tie, and fake tattoos across my knuckles that read: **G-U-N-S**. They gave me a stack of periodicals to look over before my second interview, even though I spent most of the first interview staring blankly ahead with a distant look in my eyes, as if I were harboring some terrible secret, which I was—I was really only there to infiltrate their publication.

So, while I sat on the subway flipping through page after page of gun porn—which highlighted entities such as an enhanced semi-automatic Kalashnikov shotgun bred for lightning fast domination—two things occurred to me: (1) if the FBI dropped by my apartment for a visit and found this publication on my coffee table, then I might be sent to a black site for interrogation; and (2) on the other hand, if I were searching for exactly the same assault weapon on Facebook, then I could have it shipped to me overnight.

Many people only think of Facebook as a place for dudes to cyberstalk their exes after the big breakup, but it's also the world's largest marketplace for guns. The social network advertises more assault weapons than the entire back catalog of *Tactical Weapons* magazine.

Thanks to the Internet and social media, buying guns is easier than getting a payday loan. With more than three hundred million privately owned firearms in the U.S., it's obvious that Americans love their guns more than anything but Doritos-based foodstuffs. And thanks to the National Rifle Association, nothing is going to deter their freedom to own (and acquire) massive assault rifles and Dirty Harry-caliber handguns.

Even though mass shootings in this country have become an almost daily phenomenon, the NRA defends its position by stating every possible excuse rather than the obvious: people with a history of mental health issues or suspected terrorists who are on the No Fly List should not be able to get their hands on a deadly weapon that can fire six hundred rounds per minute. For everyone but the NRA, the main source of the firearms problem is apparent: it's way too easy to buy guns in America.

In February 2017 President Trump gave a warm, helping hand to the NRA by signing a bill that rolled back an Obama-era regulation that made it harder for people with mental illnesses to purchase a gun. Apparently, twenty dead first graders at Sandy Hook were of little concern to the President. He reasoned that if you take away the guns from the mentally ill good guys, then only the mentally ill bad guys will have guns.

Once I returned home, I started to ponder the question, "Who do I 'friend' on Facebook to buy an assault rifle?" My challenge was to pose as an extremely creepy person, with cash in hand, and delve into the terrible (and lucrative) world of buying assault weapons off the Internet. Surely, some type of system of checks-and-balances must be in place to prevent an insane nut from acquiring Sandy Hook-style assault weapons?

Apparently not.

In 2013 a fifteen-year-old Kentucky boy with a loaded nine-millimeter handgun was arrested outside his school's homecoming football game. When asked where he got the gun, he replied, "Facebook."

While most sane people agree that there should be more hurdles between crazy people handing over a few hundred dollars and ownership of an AK-47, states such as Texas have decided that the unregulated sale of handguns to teenagers is an inalienable right. So much for federal background checks, which some forty percent of all gun buyers avoid by purchasing their weapons over the Internet.

That's right, federal law allows unlicensed persons to buy and sell guns without that pesky background check—no questions asked. Background checks are required only when someone attempts to purchase a gun from a federally-licensed firearms dealer.

After I surfed around like a fanboy and read about the latest attributes of Ruger's new piston-driven SR-762 AR that takes .308 Winchester cartridges, a quick Google search led me to a plethora of Facebook gun sites, such as the subtly named Guns for Sale. (There is no mincing words in that title.)

The gun-fan pages looked like the classified section of *Tactical Weapons*. I found a Bushmaster XM15-e2s AK for $800, a Bushmaster M4 "fresh from the box" for $1,200, and a Winchester 1300 Defender 12-gauge shotgun for a mere $250. A seller in South Michigan offered an LH Remington 22-250 Model 700 for $800, and as part of his pitch, he stressed that it was "not a Walmart gun!!"

But hey, it's probably a huge pain in the ass to actually buy any of these guns, right? Think again. Any of these guns can be purchased from the convenience of your smartphone.

Between Pilates classes and sending naked selfies, we are all busy people. It's such a great thing that the entire weapon-acquiring transaction can be handled discreetly and directly from the tracking device we all carry in our pockets.

To start my quest, I simply "liked" the Guns for Sale Facebook page, which featured a long quote from George Washington, the customary simple-minded proclamation from the NRA ("The only thing that will stop bad guys with guns is good guys with guns"), and almost a quarter-million followers. The Facebook page stated the rules:

> ***Post your gun for sale along with DESCRIPTION, PHOTO, PRICE and CONTACT INFO, what STATE you are in and we will repost it for millions of potential buyers to see.***

Most sellers were fine with selling to anyone. But occasionally I came across the guy who preferred to sell his enhanced semi-automatic Kalashnikov shotgun, bred for lightning fast domination, the legit way. I'm sure if you threw him an extra buck, then he'd meet you somewhere in Pittsburgh and hand it off.

After a careful perusal and consideration of my weapons needs, I inquired about an Arsenal AK-47 in excellent condition with an asking price of twelve hundred dollars, a reasonable fee for a weapon with a proven record of reliability: it was the same style rifle used in a shooting at a Carson City, Nevada IHOP restaurant that killed five people.

A man named Wade from Mooresville, North Carolina responded to my inquiry with a hard sell:

> *My AK is a very good one, it is model SLR95 milled with chrome lined barrel, muzzle break, optic sights, it is probably the most*

sought after Arsenal AK model built. circa 1995. Price is pretty firm but I can do some partial trading. Anything that goes boom interests me.

Agreeable as always, I responded that "circa 1995" was my favorite year for AK-47s and that I needed immediate shipment for "something I had planned." After some e-mail bartering, Wade provided his PayPal information and agreed to overnight shipping. "When you send the PayPal," he said, "send as a gift to a family member so I won't get a fee and neither will you!"

This was very thoughtful of Wade.

The next day, when I hadn't responded, Wade emailed back: "Ok, so what's the plan." Two days later, there was more concern: "I have someone else interested, what would you like to do?" And then: "I'll pay for the overnight shipping ..."

While pursuing assault weapons via Facebook, I learned that creepiness does not disqualify you.

Another post—"like NEW Remington 870 with tactical accessories, 12 Gauge Pump Action"—from a Facebook user, offered the very same model shotgun used by James Holmes in the movie-theater mass shooting in Aurora, Colorado. Since it's illegal to ship firearms across state lines—let alone without the benefit of an ID and background check—I made my geographically undesirable location clear to the Remington seller, who was somewhere in Texas:

I'm interested!!! I'm located in NY! I'm willing to put down a deposit. P.S. If you have any other friends who are selling guns, I want to buy them as well!

A few hours later, a man named John responded: "The gun is still available for now. I am in Texas willing to ship. The gun is in excellent condition and working perfectly ... I can do it for you for $380 and free shipping." Yay! More free shipping! And as an added convenience, John wanted to know if I would like the gun shipped straight to my home address.

I stressed to John that I needed it ASAP!

John responded, "Cool. I will get the gun packaged for now and prepare it ready for shipment."

To speed up the transaction, so that I could get my shotgun

overnight, he requested payment via Western Union, which suddenly made me wonder, "Is John a Fed?" I mean, the Internet can be a tricky place! Was I being gun-catfished? Was the U.S. government actually trying to keep people safe by enforcing the law?

Naaah.

Remembering which country I lived in, I responded:

Lot of scammers on the Internet. If I send the money, I just want to make sure I can get the Remington overnight, before my high school gets back from Spring Break.

My lack of trust seemed to hurt John's feelings. He replied:

Well, I do really understand you, I have been hurt a lot on here sir. I am not here to get hurt or to hurt anyone okay. I am honest and a serious seller and i hope you are a serious buyer as well ... Your package will be delivered ... after the payment has been made, you need not to be worried about anything ... Let me know if you are ready buy the gun now ...

Now that I had acquired a few assault weapon options, I wanted to expand my search beyond guns and into the type of bullets that would allow my guns to take down an entire SWAT team at once.

At this writing, eleven states have barred the sale or possession of armor-piercing bullets, including New York, where I live. Breaking these laws will get you anywhere from one month to ten years in prison, with fines ranging from five hundred to fifteen thousand dollars. Federal law also prohibits the manufacture, importation, and sale or delivery of armor-piercing ammunition ... unless you're on Facebook:

Selling 462 ARMOR PIERCING bullets in reloadable brass cases. These usually sell for $1.65 or more per bullet. Will sell for $700 for all or best offer. Shipping costs extra. Located in Columbus Indiana.

I emailed the seller with my customary sense of urgency: "I need armor piercing bullets! I need them shipped overnight! As many as you got! Please respond ASAP. I need them fast!"

Within a few hours, a man named Denton responded with a

delivery quote of two hundred forty-four dollars to have the bullets shipped overnight. When you gotta have armor-piercing bullets, you don't want to wait for stupid two-day Priority Mail! I replied:

That's fantastic!! I live in the Brooklyn. Very, very important that I get armor piercing bullets by Wednesday. Are they the .50 caliber— the kind that blows holes the size of hot dogs? I need as many as you got!

Surprisingly, Denton rained on my bullet parade:

I can't ship to New York. Illegal. I would be jeopardizing my shop if I did is what I was informed of by another gun shop there. Sorry.

This response almost restored my faith in law-abiding Americans, not to mention human decency. Denton, it seemed, wanted to do it by the book. Maybe the Internet's gun sellers weren't as tragically shady as I thought. Maybe Denton listened to Facebook's internal plea to regulate gun sales and delete posts that circumvented gun laws?

In a last-ditch effort, I made another armor-piercing plea:

Could you ship to North Carolina? I could fly there tonight. I'm going to be in that area to scout something out ...

Bingo! Denton replied:

Ok. If you want it shipped to North Carolina it would be there Monday or Tuesday if I ship out tomorrow. If you send money today I'll ship tomorrow. $700 and I'll cover shipping costs.

Yes! Even more free shipping! On one hand, these gun sellers were operating some of the most customer-friendly businesses I'd ever shopped at. On the other hand—holy fuck!

Two days later, after I hadn't responded, Denton e-mailed me back: "Are you interested in me sending out the ammo?"

Well, no ... but so much for the effectiveness of Facebook's self-regulation plea. Actually, it's not particularly surprising since the NRA enjoys one hundred fifty times more support on Facebook than Michael Bloomberg's "Mayors Against Illegal Guns" campaign.

But if shopping for weapons on Facebook isn't your bag, then other options are available, including Armslist, a craigslist for buying assault weapons. It's all right there in the title: it's a list of arms to buy.

Armslist is kind of like the OkCupid of weaponry. First, you set up a profile and then click on the long, hard metallic implements that attract you. Next, you try to coax the owner into letting his implement belong to you.

Armslist is so simple that even a kid can use it, although kids are not allowed (just like kids can't check out porn sites). The terms of service states that you must be eighteen years old to enter the site and buy the firearm of your dreams—and other people's nightmares. But it's the huge flippin' legal disclaimer that really brings it home. Allow me to paraphrase: *If you buy a gun off of Armslist and use it to shoot someone in the face, Armslist holds no responsibility.*

In 2011 New York City launched an investigation of private online gun sellers such as Armslist. During the sting, seventy-five of the one hundred twenty-five vendors who were contacted agreed to sell guns to people who straight-up admitted that they wouldn't pass a background check. Entering the CAPTCHA on an Internet form is harder than buying a gun off of Armslist.

I tried to set up a user name on Armslist, but my first two choices, *gunnut* and *guncrazy*, were already taken, as was the username *gunsandpussy*. So much for being clever and ironic. Finally, I settled on the username *gunsandheroin* and was ready to shop.

Posing as a disgruntled high school student who wanted to buy a "big mama of a gun" for his upcoming eighteenth birthday, I catfished and fired away at the listings, stating things such as, "I'm really into video games and want to take things to the next level."

It took all of five minutes before I received a response from a dealer trying to sell his "AR-15 Brand NEW! Plus 100 ROUNDS!!" (Two exclamation points made it easily appealing.)

"Wicked gun!!!!" I shot back via email, with lots of smiley faces included. "I'm about to turn 18 and ready to rock. AR-15s are my fav. How good is the scope? Can you see a target across a football field?"

The dealer replied: "Congrats on almost turning 18!" But then he peed on my underage gun parade: "Gotta be 21 and ship to dealer in your area."

Here was another annoying prig who seemed to obey the law when it came to firearms. So, I expressed to him that I really needed the assault rifle before school started back: "Could I get an older brother to buy it? I could bump it up and pay an extra couple hundred …"

Standing firm, he replied, "I can't legally sell you a gun." But he then informed me of a loophole: "Since it's a rifle, we won't need a bill of sale. So if you bring a friend who's over 18, I could sell it to them."

The dealer said that in order to keep things off the books he could only accept cash. There was nothing sketchy about that. All I had to do was bring a handful of cash to a disclosed meeting spot, perhaps a parking lot, and hand the money to a complete stranger who wanted to sell me a firearm. What could possibly go wrong?

I told the man that I was in summer school at my high school—where all my teachers were big dicks—and asked if I could meet him after class. Bingo—one assault weapon procured by a fictional underage minor. God bless America and the Internet.

This would have been so much funnier if it weren't so sad (and really, really, really fucking scary).

It may disturb gun control advocates to learn that any American can purchase a sizable arsenal of illegally sold guns right from their smartphone: no ID or background check required. But it's great news for kids, adults, and grandmas!

As long as the Internet exists, no one will be denied overnight shipping of a spanking new AK-47. You may, however, have to shop around a bit to find the matching armor-piercing bullets needed to blow holes the size of hot dogs through human flesh. Sleep well, America.

CHAPTER 15

IT'S A SHOTGUN WEDDING, LITERALLY

IN A TENDER FAMILY moment punctuated by loud gunfire, the lovely bride's sister observed, "Look, your ear protection matches your dress." It was a tender family moment punctuated by loud gunfire.

As the final pieces of that afternoon's nuptials were put into the chamber, a woman scattered crimson-red rose pedals on the floor of the chapel, a room usually used for gun cleaning. In a world filled with sorrow and sadness, it was refreshing to see the joy formed by the bonding of two people who were in love and shared an affinity for ... assault weapons.

The ordained minister, packing a pistol in his hip holster, addressed the young couple: "Do you, Jeff, take Sandra to be your lawfully wedded wife, to have and to hold, for better or worse, for richer or poorer, in sickness and in health, to love and cherish, from this day forward till death you do part?"

The last few words—as well as a steady spray of machine gun fire—

loudly resonated in my ears. The smell of gunpowder lingered in my nostrils as the blast of assault weapons, which popped from the shooting range in the next room, peppered the wedding vows.

Couples that spray together stay together. Gun nuts in love have found their sanctuary in America's firearm-obsessed society. Soulmates can leap into matrimony while standing in the line of fire. The Gun Store was the first establishment in Las Vegas to offer literal Shotgun Weddings. Couples are married inside the weaponry outlet and seal their vows by firing off AK-47s, Uzis, or the same MP5 submachine guns used by SWAT teams. It's a ceremony that would easily secure the NRA's Second Amendment stamp of wedlock approval.

You can pry my gun from my cold dead hands and then slap a wedding ring on my finger. These Shotgun Weddings are as American as baseball, apple pie, and mass schoolyard shootings. Guys no longer have to dodge the bullet of marriage—when real ammunition is involved. The only thing that would make these nuptials more patriotic is if baby Jesus conducted the ceremony himself.

"It's loud. They duck sometimes," said Emily Couture, who came up with the wedding/firearms idea in 2011. Emily, who also acts as the Gun Store's media person, claimed that she went to her boss and said, "Let's do weddings." But he looked at her like she was a crazy person.

Imagine that. Such a lack of vision!

Emily put the hammer down, became an ordained minister, and declared herself a marriage officiant. Recalling her first wedding at the Gun Store, she said, "We let them get married downrange where the guns were shot. And then they actually got to shoot downrange where they just got married twenty minutes earlier."

Since Vegas is the wedding capital of the world, Emily's idea fits nicely into the other genre-specific weddings offered in Sin City, such as a Monster Mini Golf KISS (yes, the makeup-wearing band) ceremony, a mafioso-themed union at The Mob Museum, or an Ilsa She Wolf of the SS wedding, based on the eponymous 1975 Nazisploitation and sexploitation film directed by Don Edmond. "If they want to get married at a gun range holding a big fat Uzi," she said, "far be it for me to keep them from it."

So true! Because if you take assault weapon weddings away from the good guys, then only the bad guys will be having assault weapon weddings.

For true gun-crazy couples, the Mr. & Mrs. Smith & Wesson

package offers more guns, ammunition, and targets—with irony delivered tragically when things sour and they shoot each other. The five hundred dollar package includes the legal paperwork, wedding ceremony, gift bag, VIP shooting range access, and five shotgun blasts for both bride and groom.

Tying the knot in a high-caliber ceremony presents amusing antidotes. Emily recalled one couple who had packed their friends and entire family into the gun range chapel. When it came time for the vows, machine gun fire erupted from the next range. "And instead of saying 'I do,'" Emily said, "the bride screams, 'Holy shit!'" Once the laughter died down, Emily reassured the bride: "We're all safe. The bullets won't come through the walls. It's a gun range, so it's loud."

According to Melissa, the woman in the back of the room in charge of cueing the ceremony music, crying often accompanies Shotgun Weddings: "Out of the three weddings I've done, two of them have ended in tears." No, those tears weren't caused by a stray bullet shell flying into someone's eye; they were tears of pure elation, something that only a true romantic encounters when they're choked up with emotion from holy matrimony that has been sealed inside a gun range with a blast of bullets.

That day's Shotgun Wedding couple hailed from Canada. The amorous pair had been together for twelve years, and now, finally, they were romantically ready to lock-and-load like true conservative Americans.

"We're here because people love each other and guns," Emily summarized. "Guns don't have to be about anger and hate."

Since foreigners want to embrace America's gun culture—and take part in what is not legally permitted within their borders—the Gun Store has married numerous couples from Canada and the UK. Contrary to what you might expect, not a single wedding was canceled after shooting tragedies such as the Sandy Hook massacre. In fact, bookings actually increased. Perhaps, like the Oath Keepers, they feared that the government would soon take away an individual's God-given right to an assault weapon-themed nuptial and force citizens—after the round-up—to marry in 24/7 FEMA camps. Now that would be a shitty wedding.

The wedding party of eight—all shining with that healthy Canadian glow—arrived in formal attire: suits and ties for the men and long black dresses for the women. A white trellis, covered in flowers and

IT'S A SHOTGUN WEDDING, LITERALLY   153

a mounted Uzi and Tommy gun, rested on a makeshift stage. Family members sat in grey foldout chairs, ready to witness that special day.

Before the ceremony, the nervous groom—sharply dressed with a traditional floral boutonnière in his jacket lapel—shared his story: "We were looking for a vacation for my fiancée's birthday, and at the spur of the moment, we said, 'Why don't we just get married while we're in Vegas?'" With no recoil, he expressed pride in their decision to put the bolt action down. "It seemed like good timing."

Things then got serious. Classical music—emanating from a CD player—filled the chapel. The lovely bride, adorned in a long and flowing beige dress, entered. A hush fell upon the room before a barrage of gunplay erupted from the next room: POP-POP-POP!

"I give you this ring as an eternal symbol of my love and commitment to you," recited the groom. The words were hard to hear over the steady POP-POP-POP of gunfire.

"By the power invested in me by the State of Nevada, I now pronounce you husband and wife!"

Kisses. Claps. Gunfire. Tears. More gunfire.

Personally, I was disappointed that—instead of rice—handfuls of bullets weren't flung directly at the happy wedding couple. The bride's mother cried in unison with the echoing bullet blasts. But unlike other scenarios where bullet blasts lead to crying people, these tears were full of joy.

"Will you hold my flowers?" asked the bride as she exchanged her bouquet for an assault weapon. The entire wedding party snapped photos under the trellis and traded off machine guns with each other. Mom and Dad took turns cradling an AK-47. It looked like someone was about to have a new Facebook profile photo.

"I don't know if I'm holding it properly," said the proud mom, clumsily nestling the assault weapon.

With the ceremony complete, eye and ear protection was dispersed amongst the formally-clad wedding party. They moved down the hall—past a range of ordinary shooters—to the special VIP shooting range, adorned with marble floors. The couple was ready to consummate their marriage with a loud BANG—literally. I hoped there weren't going be any arguments that might have needed to be settled in a messy way.

Ground rules were laid out to prevent minor mishaps, such as a dead groom. For example, the newlyweds weren't allowed to throw the bouquet in the air and riddle it with bullets, even though this type of gunplay was often requested. "We'll definitely hang up your bouquet and you can shoot that downrange," Emily explained. "You can shoot whatever you want."

The range master, on hand like a waiter, loaded the weapons and served the new husband and wife an array of firearms to blast their way into the explosive world of marriage.

The Gun Store conducts an average of five weddings per month and offers any type of weaponry-themed wedding that's possible—and legal. Some couples have been married ironically with a redneck theme, and other couples have dressed up like hillbillies (yes, there is a difference between rednecks and hillbillies). But the one thing that's not allowed: if it's a real shotgun wedding, then the pregnant bride cannot shoot since the sound reverberations from a MP-40 might adversely affect the child in the womb.

When the Gun Store conducted its first real shotgun, Shotgun Wedding, which was booked before the bride became pregnant, she cried afterwards, but not because she was moved by the ceremony—she had to wait in the lobby while her wedding party fired semi-automatics.

"The weirdest phone call I've gotten is a request to do a nudist wedding, which we're down with," Emily said. As long as the credit card is approved, they're good to go. "They could have a full nudist wedding and shoot nude." The Gun Store, however, doesn't supply genital protection for nude newlyweds. "If brass that flies and melts them and burns them," she added, "that's on them."

Ever adaptive to cultural trends and alternative lifestyles, Emily recently administered her first shrapnel-infused same-sex marriage. The couple, locals from Las Vegas, was thrilled that they could legally express their love for each other with weapons. Though, in the era of Trump, gay people better rush out for their Shotgun Weddings before The Donald and Gorsuch try to overturn Obergefell v. Hodges and same-sex marriage—with or without guns—once again becomes illegal in America.

Helping gun-centric wedding planners, Trump's election victory increased gun sales, which can be partially attributed to his backing by the NRA as a result of his opposition to limiting the Second Amendment's right to bear arms, including stricter background checks.

But in trigger-happy America, not everyone is thrilled with the prospect of Shotgun Weddings; some grumpy-faced meanies want to rain on these bullet-riddled wedding days. They feel that it's mentally and emotionally harmful for people to love firearms so much that they must be included in their wedding vows.

According to Jonathan Hutson, spokesman for the Brady Campaign to Prevent Gun Violence, responsible gun owners "appreciate the risks of having a gun. They don't treat a gun casually, like a party favor."

Maybe Hutson is overlooking the original draft of the Constitution, where the Second Amendment specified that a "well regulated Militia, being necessary to the security of a free State, the right of the people to keep and bear Arms, and the right of those who want to seal their wedding vows by firing off assault weapons, shall not be infringed."

For Ladd Everitt, communications director for the Coalition to Stop Gun Violence in Washington, D.C., American culture is part of the problem. "We live in a society where a certain subset of gun owners fetishizes firearms, taking them as something akin to religious idols," he said. "There is a strong spiritual element here, where commonly embraced maxims of faith—thou shalt not kill, thou shalt have no other gods before me—are rejected outright. The gun culture takes great pride in ignoring the risks posed by firearms, and embraces the suffering they cause: that's the price of liberty. Some might describe this philosophy as nihilism."

And everyone knows what happens when nihilism takes over in a relationship: the love goes flat, which is why the Gun Store hosts divorce parties. On the same day a divorce was finalized, a group of women, dressed in all black, showed up at the range. "They came in and had pictures of her ex that they took out of the frame," said Emily. "And it was a contest to see who could shoot pictures of the ex-husband ...We don't encourage that."

Afterwards, when the divorcée saw the bullet-riddled photos of her former husband's face, she remarked, "Wow, that's cheaper than therapy." And less time consuming than prison.

I witnessed a more joyous occasion. "Make sure your firearm is pointed that way," said the range master to the bride while gesturing in the opposite direction of the wedding party. "We have both automatic and fully automatic. As long as you keep your finger on that trigger, it will keep firing rounds."

The range master presented the newlyweds with a menu of firearms. "I'll definitely take an AK-47, and you should have an Uzi," said the happy groom, gunsplaining to his wife.

"So, is everybody shooting something?" asked the bride of her sister.

"I think mom is. I'm still thinking about it," she replied, letting out a nervous laugh. "I'm not sure."

As the lovely bride fired her Benelli into a zombie target, wedding party members cringed with each passing shot. Mom shrieked, and my teeth began to hurt from the blasts.

Then, the range master piped in: "One thing I like to do is have you guys share a lane together so you can enjoy watching each other shoot. To start off the marriage appropriately, you guys get to start sharing right away. That's the whole idea."

The happy newlyweds proceeded to finalize their vows by blowing away Nazi zombies—the most popular target for newlyweds—with semi-automatic shotguns, blasting holes the size of softballs into the targets. Then, they moved onto pistols and Uzis. Finally, the pristine bride, still in her flowing wedding dress, wrapped her hands firmly around an AK-47.

"All right! It's legal now," said the groom after firing away at the final target.

After shooting all that weaponry, the couple was pumped with adrenaline. The loving bride looked adoringly at her new husband.

"Any words of wisdom on starting a new life?" I asked her.

"Hopefully, it's not as violent as it is today," she said laughing.

Emily put the wedding into context, claiming that "our couples are more trusting" since "they come and get married around firearms. I think they have a solid shot because they trust each other with their lives." She optimistically added, "The couple that shoots together stays together."

As the saying goes, marriage is for life, until death us do part. But more than half of the time, the weapon used to carry out an "intimate partner" homicide—when a person kills a spouse, boyfriend or girlfriend, or someone with whom they previously had a romantic relationship—is a gun. Let's pray that these shotgun marriages don't end the same way they began.

MAKING AMERICA GREAT AGAIN

PART FIVE

INTRODUCTION

THE TSUNAMI IS COMING

YOU CAN TELL A lot about the state of a country by comparing the state of its public and private infrastructure. Take a look—if you can sneak past the gated community guard shack and peek through the privets without getting tackled by a rent-a-goon—at the homes of the wealthy.

Note the manicured lawns of the one-percenters, fertilized the months recommended by experts, painstakingly controlled for weeds, and irrigated on timers calibrated by volume. Check out the garden: lines of shrubs that run a hundred bucks each and red-dyed mulch that hides the dirty brown dirt while tamping down unwanted dandelions before they get a chance to sprout. The driveways are flat, smooth, and free of cracks. Stucco walls, if you live out West, are similarly crack-free; if you're east of the Mississippi, bricks are framed by perfect pointing. Every detail, from the brass numbers on the mailbox to the baseboards to the perfect absence of cobwebs in high ceiling corners, reflects thorough, routine, and frequent maintenance and repairs by a retinue of professional service providers. Tasteful. New. Kept up.

Bear in mind: all this perfectly-maintained stuff houses a single family. At most, we're talking two parents, four kids, and a nanny or two. Certainly fewer than ten people.

Now look at our public infrastructure.

Drive on a public highway in any major city: New York, Chicago, Los Angeles. It's a disaster. Potholes so big you worry about breaking an axle. (And you should. In New York State, for example, a recent study estimated that bad roads and bridges cost motorists twenty billion three hundred million dollars annually in repairs.) There's cracked concrete and asphalt, missing guardrails, stolen signs, and everywhere you turn, garbage. Graffiti and vandalism take a toll, but mostly, it's all just old: rusted and worn out after years of "deferred maintenance"—i.e., none at all. Yeah, people throw crap out their car windows, but municipal governments don't clean it up for days, weeks, even months at a time.

Connecting two of NYC's biggest boroughs, the Brooklyn-Queens Expressway is used daily by one hundred sixty thousand vehicles. It is hideous. It is narrow. It is literally falling apart—constantly. "With its multitude of trucks and dangerous on-ramps, the BQE is a den of congestion at virtually all hours of the day," *The New York Times* reported in 2012. "But one factor has condemned this antiquated 16.8-mile stretch of highway to a place of longstanding infamy in the New York metropolitan area, if not all of urban America: construction that never seems to end. As Gerry Michalowski, a truck driver who has traveled the BQE since 1978, put it, 'It was under construction then, and it's still under construction now.'"

That well-maintained, pristine house I mentioned earlier is used by only a half a dozen people per year; the BQE is used by fifty-eight million vehicles each year.

If you don't think there's something wrong with this picture—if you defend the "right" of the wealthy to aggregate more and more until the point when they own everything including our bodies and souls—then consider this: rich people have to drive on those roads too. By definition, five hundred eighty thousand of those BQE vehicles are operated by one-percenters.

America isn't broke, but most Americans are. The reason is simple: too few people have too much of our national wealth. The pauperizing of our common property—the deliberate starving of public funding for roads, bridges, parks, schools, and public hospitals (even hospitals charged with caring for veterans of America's oil wars)—reflects the economic and political system's ass-backward priorities. It's immoral—because any society that spends more resources to maintain and upgrade private homes than public works is crazy stupid.

And it hurts the economy.

The American Society of Civil Engineers estimates that the United States needs to spend three trillion six hundred billion dollars over the next six years to replace and repair the nation's decaying dams and rusting water mains; overhaul its parks and outdated schools; and upgrade crumbling airports, train and bus terminals, roads, and bridges—many of which have deteriorated to Third World standards. (Although, to be fair to the Third World, I've seen U.S.-funded roads in Afghanistan in better shape than some in L.A.)

The ASCE gives the U.S. a D+ grade on infrastructure, and the World Economic Forum ranks the U.S. twenty-fifth in the world in infrastructure, behind Oman, Saudi Arabia, and Barbados.

It doesn't have to be this way.

Josef Stalin, of all people, showed how infrastructure could be prioritized over private property. The dictator approved every extravagance—and why not? U.S. Presidents sign off on every luxury the military dreams up.

Determined that his new Moscow Metro be a "palace of the people" for the Soviet capital's subway commuters, Stalin ordered that no expense be spared to create a system that was not only fast and efficient but beautiful. "In stark contrast to the gray city above," *The Times* wrote as late as 1988, "the bustling, graffiti-less Metro is a subterranean sanctuary adorned with crystal chandeliers, marble floors and skillfully crafted mosaics and frescoes fit for a czar's palace." Of course, the chandeliers were ripped out of the czar's old palaces and moved underground; for future stations more stunning ones were designed from scratch using radically innovative techniques.

The Moscow Metro remains a showcase of what socialism could do at its best: prioritize the people and thus improve their daily lives.

But socialism isn't in the cards, not yet anyway. All we have now is the two-party system. You may not like it (and I certainly don't), but it's unsurprising that people disgusted by the Republican Party for allowing Donald Trump to become its nominee and then president would naturally turn to the Democrats as the most obvious viable political alternative. But the weirdness in the GOP shouldn't distract us from the fact that the Democrats have gotten themselves into one hell of a fractured mess—and it would take a lot of work to restore it to a party that could win elections and govern again.

In the 1970s, when I was a kid, I asked my mother to explain the difference between the two major parties. "Democrats," she explained, "are the party of the working man. Republicans represent big business."

She was a Democrat, obviously. Still, I'm sure Republican families had their version of my mom's binary, perhaps something along the lines of: "Republicans believe in less government and more hard work. Democrats want high taxes and welfare."

The two-party system was easy to understand.

Now, it's a muddled mess—especially if you're a Democrat.

Today's Democratic Party relies on big corporations, especially big Wall Street investment banks, for campaign donations. The old alliance between the party and labor unions is dead. Democrats support trade deals that hurt American workers. When the economy tanked at the end of the last decade, President Obama left laid-off workers and foreclosed-upon homeowners twisting in the wind; he bailed out the banks instead. Hillary Clinton, who supported the TPP trade deal before she was against it, promised bankers that she'd be their friend if she won. Whatever the Democrats are now, they're not the party of working Americans.

So what is the Democratic Party now? What does it stand for and against?

I honestly don't know, and I'm obsessed with politics. So if I don't know what Democrats want, it's a safe bet no one else does, either.

"It's all well and good—and really very satisfying—to harp constantly about the terribleness of Donald Trump," observed *New York Times* columnist Gail Collins. "But people need to see the Democratic line on the ballot and think of something more than Not as Dreadful."

Yes they do.

Failure to articulate an affirmative vision of what she was for, not just against, was largely to blame for Hillary Clinton's devastating defeat. **Trump Is Evil and Dangerous** wasn't enough to win in 2016. Yet party leaders still haven't begun to say how they would address the problems voters care about, like healthcare.

The Clintonistas, still in charge of the Democratic Party despite their incompetent stewardship, believe that Obamacare will survive because the Republicans' Trumpcare alternative is unpopular, even with Republicans. But they're wrong. In one out of three counties, there is only one insurance company in the local healthcare "exchange." Zero competition guarantees skyrocketing premiums and shrinking benefits. The collapse of Obamacare makes healthcare the number one concern for American voters.

What would Democrats do about healthcare if they were in charge? As far as I can tell, nada.

House Democratic Leader Nancy Pelosi's website brags about Obamacare and its achievements. "House Democrats," it says, "continually work to implement and improve health care reform to ensure that the best healthcare system in the world only gets better." Newsflash to Ms. Pelosi: the U.S., actually, has the worst healthcare system in the developed world.

When it comes to healthcare, Democrats are just like the Republicans on global warming: they won't admit there's a problem. So how can they offer a solution? They don't.

Even though fifty-eight percent of American voters want a European-style, taxpayer-subsidized, single-payer system, the Democratic Party platform does not propose significant reforms to Obamacare.

The wreckage of deindustrialization in the nation's heartland is widely viewed as key to Trump's surprise win. So what is the Democrats' plan to create jobs, increase wages, and help victims of the opioid epidemic?

Aside from "Trump sucks," Democrats don't much to say.

"We will create jobs that stay in America and restore opportunity for all Americans, starting with raising the minimum wage, expanding Pell grants and making college tuition tax deductible," the party said in a statement a few days before Election Day 2016. Sounds great! But details are hard to come by.

In 2016 when it mattered, two hundred twenty-five thousand dollar-a-speech Hillary asked workers to settle for a minimum wage of twelve dollars per hour. Now, finally, Democrats are officially endorsing Bernie Sanders' fifteen dollars per hour. But it really should be at least twenty-two dollars per hour. And anyway, how would a minimum wage increase, or additional Pell grants, or even tax-deductible tuition "create jobs?" They wouldn't. We need a big, WPA-style federal hiring program and a law mandating that evil outsourcing companies start hiring Americans. But the Dems won't get behind that either.

When Democrats do have something to say, it's trivial and small-bore, like making college tuition tax deductible. Why not go big? Did you know that the U.S. could make four-year college tuition-free for the price of the ongoing war against Iraq?

Why are the Democrats so lame? Suspect number one is the lingering rift between the Sanders and Clinton wings of the party. "There is this grassroots movement voters' arm of the party, and the more corporate, institutional part of the party. And the movement arm is tired of the institutional part telling us the only place for us is in the streets," said Nebraska Democratic Party Chairwoman Jane Kleeb, a Sanders supporter. A party split by a civil war between a populist-left and a corporatist-right can't articulate an inspiring platform of exciting solutions to American's big problems. A purge, or a schism, would fix this.

Trump is already one of the most unpopular presidents in history. Going against him ought to be easy. But Democrats are about to find out—again—that people won't vote for you unless you give them a good reason to get off their couches and drive on the pothole-filled roads to the polls.

If you're a Bernie Sanders Democrat, you have to be a complete idiot to believe that the Democratic Party has learned the lesson of 2016: lean left or go home. Even after it became clear that Trump was putting together the most right-wing administration in American history, Democrats were still voting in favor of Republican appointees.

Given the escalating rage of the party's progressive base in the Age of Trump and the absolute refusal of the DNC leadership to grant them concessions, it's hard to imagine this restive crowd staying calm and keeping Democratic.

The tsunami is coming. Lefties have a choice: get washed away or grab a surfboard. In the meantime, Americans continue to watch their infrastructure collapse, their paychecks shrink, and their dreams evaporate.

–Ted Rall

As dreams evaporate for many, **HARMON** infiltrates some laborers still searching for a better America ...

CHAPTER 16

HERE COMES THE REPO MAN

It was an ordinary ninety-degree Monday in blistering hot August. Pawnshop after pawnshop—or gamblers' procession museums—lined the streets of recession-casualty Reno, Nevada. Bankruptcy billboards trumpeted: *MONEY TO LOAN. WE ACCEPT FOOD STAMPS. NO APPOINTMENT NECESSARY!* Outside the Grand Sierra casino, a huge video marquee blazoned the words *ANOTHER LUCKY WINNER—CAROL S. $34,500*. The large image of a smiling old woman announced to ordinary people that it was possible to strike it rich.

This town is home to *deplorableness*—that sense of grinding whiteman's dispossession that led to Donald Trump's stunning victory ... stunning to those who don't spend time in places like this.

"The security guard here hates me," declared Brian Turley, a chubby guy with a cherub face and goatee. He laughed as I climbed into his massive, red tow truck to ride shotgun. "If they see me, they'll try to kick me out."

It can't be good for business when the cars of casino patrons are repossessed from the parking lot while they're inside gambling away their monthly loan payments.

Since the Great Recession, the repo business has become a thriving boom industry. "Put it this way—we haven't died down in two years," Brian said as he chugged a Red Bull before starting his 3 p.m. to midnight shift. "It sucks. It's unfortunate. What can you do? Everyone is having a rough time."

With the economy still recovering for many people, the repossession trade is a booming industry that often claims the vehicles of Trump supporters whose lives he promised to make better.

Brian landed the job of repo man—a legal car thief—without even knowing how to drive a tow truck. After graduating from college in Reno with dreams of becoming a teacher, his career plans took a curve with the economy.

"It was just a money issue," he explained. "I wasn't making enough working a dead-end job in a warehouse. I knew I was going to make more as a repo man than as a teacher."

A repo man, who works on commission, can typically earn between fifty and seventy-five dollars per car. But even the repo biz is subject to the depredations of avaricious capitalists trying to make more for themselves at the expense of their workers. As a result, many companies have turned to an hourly pay structure, which is dictated by region, cost of living, and state regulatory issues.

For Brian, fortune took a spin for the better after he played on the same softball team as Justin Zane, the repo boss of Zane Investigations, Inc. "One night I was drunk and said, 'I want to go on a repo and see what it's all about,'" Brian told me. "I've been hooked ever since."

As various lock-picking tools of the repo trade—Slim Jims, wedges, etc.—clanked on the dashboard, I asked him, "So, what hooks you?"

With a sly smile, Brian replied, "You get to do things people normally don't get to do. It's not every day you get to drive up to someone's house and say, 'I'm here for your car.'" He once seized twelve cars in one day!

In addition to cars, Brian has also repoed boats, motorcycles, Jet Skis, motor homes, and a tanning bed. In a sign of these desperate times, the tiny city of Reno boasts a whopping five repo companies, with Zane Investigations running six repo trucks and seizing unpaid vehicles for thirty to forty different banks.

"We handle things differently from other agencies. We won't get into a pissing match. You don't want to add fuel to the fire," he said, sounding a lot like Harry Dean Stanton's character in *Repo Man*. "People fall into unfortunate circumstances—there's no work here. It doesn't help to call them a loser or a deadbeat. You've just got to know how to talk to people."

Despite Brian's laid-back and likable demeanor, the job isn't easy. "Everyone thinks we're the bad guys," he said while looking up an address on a laptop mounted by the front dash. "If nobody's repoing cars, your auto loan would be at forty percent. I'm just a guy doing my job." As, of course, was Himmler.

The address was in a low-income Hispanic neighborhood. "I've been here many times. I knew this guy was going to live down here. We do a lot of repos in this area," Brian said. "I talked to him last week on the phone, and he said, 'Fuck you. I'm not going to pay it, and you're not taking my Chevy.' All this for a '96 Chevy Silverado piece of shit."

Noting that the neighborhood contained large dogs in backyards, houses with **FOR RENT** signs, and heads suspiciously looking out of windows, I asked Brian, "So what's the process?"

Brian explained that repossession was always the last resort. "A customer buys a car. They fall delinquent on their payments. The bank calls for a repo order," he said. "We start with their last known address. Chances are they got evicted or did a midnight run. If they have no phone, then we'll go to their place of employment."

I asked what happens when he finds out where they live. "We seize the vehicle from their property. If the car's there and I can hook it, we'll take it," Brain said. After a brief pause, he continued, "They usually come out screaming."

Typically, it's a long shot to find a car at someone's home during work hours, but we had just struck repo gold.

"That's it!" Brian said, as if he were a kid on Christmas morning. The Silverado—naively parked in full view—sat in front of a house (rookie error) with an unruly lawn and an ominous **KEEP OUT** sign. We were about to take the truck from its owner.

Brian swiftly backed up his tow truck to the maroon Chevy and maneuvered a mechanized sling under the car, hooking it onto the frame. Though a bit chubby, he moved with ninja-like proficiency, traveling at four times his normal speed, and secured the vehicle in less time than it takes to load a gun.

Enter the aforementioned truck owner, a mustachioed Hispanic man wearing a tank top. He stormed out of the garage with fire in his eyes, swearing in Spanish. He was the kind of guy that Trump would like to deport: a hardworking family man.

"That's the guy who told me to go fuck myself a few days ago," Brian confirmed. But this battle was a no-win scenario for the man.

Moments later, a small child who was speaking in English appeared by the man's side. Brian said to the little boy, "Tell him he has to make his account current. Then, he'll get it back."

As the Silverado was clamped down and raised by the tow truck, the disgraced ex-motorist removed the license plates: the only souvenir of his fallen American dream. This whole interaction made me feel like crying.

"Do you think he'll pay it back?" I asked Brian as we pulled away with the vehicle and merged into heavy traffic.

"No," blurted out Brian. "It's just a gut feeling."

Out of both curiosity and personal-safety concerns (including my own), I asked, "How dangerous does this get?"

Brian replied, "I've had two guns pulled on me ... and an ax."

An ax?

"Yeah. And he was a big guy," Brian said. "I was out in the middle of nowhere, on a ranch. The wife didn't tell the husband that she took out a title loan. When we went to hook up the car, he came running out with an ax. He told me I was trespassing."

Brian informed the man that he would leave but also added that he would be taking the car with him. "He called the cops," Brian said. "They told him, 'There's nothing we can do.'"

While thinking that parts of Reno still resembled the Wild West, I asked him, "And people have pulled guns on you?"

Brian said that on his first or second night of training a guy came out of his house brandishing a gun. "He was drunk as shit," Brian recalled. "We knocked on his door and nothing happened. We were hooking up the car, and this skinny dude came out yelling and screaming, 'You're not taking my car!'"

Brian mimed holding a gun at my head and said, "He was doing this with the gun. I didn't know whether I wanted to do this after that."

Now uncomfortable, I shifted in my seat and mumbled, "I know exactly how you feel." But there was no time to dwell on my fears.

"Holy shit! That's my Hummer!" screamed Brian as an H2 barreled down the road, traveling in the opposite direction.

"How can you tell?" I asked him.

He replied, "I've repoed it before!"

After pulling a screeching U-turn at the next intersection, we were now in hot pursuit of the Hummer. Yeehaw! Reno's crumbling housing market had put up for repo some poor real estate guy's idiotic and oversized status symbol.

"What's the plan?" I asked, noting that the towed Silverado was still clunking behind us.

"If we get to his house, I'll block him in the driveway," said Brian, intensely focused on the massive Hummer as it wove through traffic ahead of us. Perhaps, I thought, it would have been easier for its owner to make payments on a more gas-efficient vehicle.

We would have to wait for another day for that repo. The H2 gave us the slip at the next stoplight and disappeared into Reno's rush hour.

"He's going home, and he's going to lock it in the garage," said Brian, shaking his head, well aware of the scenario. "There are three types of people you repo. There's the ones who know it's coming: they'll clean out their car for you. There's the ones who hide their car. And there's the ones who put up a fight."

Near a development of new houses, most of which were in foreclosure, empty billboards dotted the barren landscape. While tuning the radio to a classic-rock station, Brian said, "Once work died down in the construction boom, all these people got stuck. They woke up one morning and there was no work.

"I repoed an entire fleet of cars from a construction company when the economy collapsed. They were in business for thirty-five years with three hundred fifty employees. No work. I did feel bad for those guys."

Back at the repo company's office, Brian opened a chain-link fence that surrounded the lot and said, "What sucks is when people try to keep their heads above water and can't."

He recalled an old Mexican guy whose car he repoed. The man worked three different jobs just to survive. "'I'm scrubbing toilets. I'm working as a janitor after I work construction,' he told me. 'I either pay for my car or I pay rent. I have three hundred dollars to my name,'" said Brian. It's the elderly—or single moms who aren't getting child support—that really get to him.

Filled with dozens of cars, motorcycles, motor homes, and even a golf cart, the one-and-a-half-acre repo yard was a graveyard of financial wreckage and despair.

"About four people come back to get them a week," Brian told me. Typically, the bank holds on to a car for ten days: the window in which a customer has the chance to get their car back. If a payment is not made, the car ends up at auction.

"It's unfortunate to see how busy we're getting, especially when you've got people trying to find work. And they just can't," said Brian. "When I first started, the economy wasn't real bad—like it is now."

As we left the office and headed farther from town into the belly of rural darkness, Brian admitted, "When I first started, I got the jitters. The first four or five cars—I had to deal with a lot of drunk-asses. You can get into a bad situation really fast."

Noting a cluster of lights ahead that broke the darkness, I asked him, "So how do you handle it?"

He said that he tries to defuse the situation. "Let them go through their yelling stage. Let them cry," he advised. "It's no different from a kid having a temper tantrum. Once they're through, I explain what they need to do to get their car back."

As we turned into a quiet and dark neighborhood, the suburban version of the American Dream was about to come crashing down. "We got a doubleheader: two cars at the same address," Brian explained with a small amount of delight. "We're going after a Trailblazer and a Yukon. The Trailblazer just turned over."

In this subdivision, American flags hung from porches, families huddled comfortably in their homes, and lights flickered from TV sets. The only sound was the low hum of the repo man's tow truck. We slowly passed a two-story house with a kiddie pool and toys littering its walkway.

"There's the Yukon! And the Trailblazer is right in front!" screamed Brian. Nervous adrenaline pumped inside me as he called for backup. "Jared will take the Yukon, and I'll take the Trailblazer. Both of them are going to go!"

Brian parked the tow truck a few blocks away. We jumped out and walked silently, but swiftly, through the pitch-black neighborhood. Using tactics employed by real car thieves, we were about to legally steal both of these cars. It's no wonder some people have come running out of their houses swinging axes.

In the window, the silhouette of a mom's head was illuminated only by the light of a glaring TV. Brian quickly flipped on his flashlight and confirmed the VIN on each vehicle.

"It's them!" he whispered as we walked stealthily back to the tow truck and hopped inside. "Now we wait."

Knots twisted in my stomach. My heart pounded, and my palms sweated. As I spotted a black cat crossing the road, my mind raced through all the possible outcomes of this situation, most of which were extremely bad. I wondered what creative weapon might be used to ward off the repo man.

"Do you get nervous?" I asked, breaking the heavy silence.

"No, I get antsy, Brian said. "I just want to get this fucking car so I can get another one."

Trying to seem like I was totally into this, I asked him, "What's the game plan?"

Without delay, Brian responded, "Hook 'em up and wait for them to come out. It probably won't go over very well. They probably will be really fucking pissed. We are taking both their cars.

"I imagine this guy's going to come out of his house and go, 'What the fuck?' But it's the nature of things. You never know people. They could be the nicest people in the world or world-class motherfuckers. We'll find out in five minutes."

As the waiting continued, I pondered whether or not this was the stupidest thing that I'd ever done, which truly would've been something. Then Jared—a heavily-tattooed guy whose dog rode shotgun with him in the tow truck—finally arrived. The once quiet neighborhood was now filled with the foreign hum of two tow-truck engines.

"I'll go in first," relayed Brian as if he were a general leading his troops into repo battle. "The Trailblazer is in front of the house, and the Yukon is in the driveway."

We moved out. I pretended that we were being accompanied by the strains of Wagner's "Ride of the Valkyries." Within seconds, we were in front of the house and at work on both the Trailblazer and the Yukon. As the vehicles were lifted off the ground in wide view of the neighborhood, movable parts clanked loudly. I wondered about Nevada's gun laws—very pro-gun, I presumed.

First, a shirtless and tattooed neighbor with a hanging beer belly emerged from behind a trailer in the driveway. He looked like the kind of guy that you'd see on *Cops*.

"Are you guys repoing those?" he asked, unfazed by the drama. Then, someone in the quiet suburban home abruptly flipped on a light, and a frantic, pudgy woman came running outside. She cried into a cellphone, "Honey, they're taking the cars! Both of them!"

As her sobs rung through the neighborhood, it was no longer silent. The economy had claimed another casualty.

"Our payment's not due until the twenty-sixth," she tearfully pleaded.

Brian remained patient, informing her that she needed to contact the dealership that provided the loan. "You have ten days to get it back," he assured her.

Jared and Brian helped the woman empty her belongings from both cars. Toys, dolls, and a child's car seat were shoved into garbage bags.

"It's not the end of the world," Jared solemnly assured her as he put another handful of dolls into a garbage bag.

"I'm freaking out!" the woman cried loudly. "It's my only car! And I have a son in a wheelchair!"

A Hiroshima bomb-sized depression raced through me when the woman turned to me to plead her case. I looked down, not knowing what to say. Tears flowed into the river of recession.

The Yukon was now clamped down; so was the Trailblazer. As the last remains of baby toys were pulled from the vehicles, the woman suddenly broke into a crazed, awkward laugh.

"We wanted them to come get this one," she said twice, referring to the Trailblazer. "We're ten payments behind."

There were no axes or guns. But after popping the trucks, it began to feel as if people had been expecting the repo man to come and seize status symbols they could never afford, bought with loans they could never repay.

Next, we were off to Blue Sage Court, a neighborhood in Stead, Nevada near a power plant and adjacent to a huge, empty field where one might expect to find on occasion a corpse or two. As we hooked up a Jeep Liberty, which was parked in the driveway of another victim's house, the bathrobe-clad next-door neighbor—who appeared to have been drinking beer in her garage—ran to alert the home's occupants. Dogs began to bark loudly, and a few moments later, a large bald guy, with a worried face, emerged. A big-haired woman stood by his side. "My wife just lost her job a week ago. I can pay half," he kept repeating. "I just can't pay the full amount. I made a five hundred dollar payment last week."

Once again, Brian patiently told the poor guy what to do. They didn't resist as the Jeep was towed away. I mean, what was next to go? The tanning bed? The house? Their sanity?

"Stead just got bitch-slapped," he said over the phone as we drove away. After all, Brian was just a guy who was doing his job during life in wartime Reno. "All in all, it's been a pretty good day."

CHAPTER 17

FEAR & LOATHING BENEATH LAS VEGAS

FOUR HUNDRED FIFTY MILES southeast of Reno, beneath a city that epitomizes opulence and excess, the beam of my flashlight illuminated a large, anguished face with the scrawled words, *I Am Not Well*. This self-portrait and other eerie graffiti, all done with child-like skill, lined the walls. Another passage served as a permanent reminder to its author's tortured humanity: *I think of myself as an intelligent human with the soul of a clown, which forces me to blow it at most important moments.* It was a strange feeling to witness a person living in worse conditions than a wild animal.

"When I first came down, it was packed. There were a lot of people—families, women, about twelve guys," recalled John, a middle-aged man from Orlando, Florida. Huddled beneath a tarp that sheltered him and a shopping cart full of possessions, John estimated that ninety percent of the tunnel population suffers from addiction problems: drugs, alcohol, and/or gambling. The others, who are mentally ill or lost their jobs, had nowhere else to go but down.

Where great wealth occurs, there is almost always great poverty. And no city sells the dream of acquiring wealth as quickly and painlessly as Las Vegas.

"I've been living in here almost two years," said John as he looked towards the beam of my flashlight.

Directly below the glamorous Las Vegas Strip exists a level of deprivation and depredation that even many long-time residents of America's gambling capital have rarely seen: a series of dark flood tunnels that house roughly a thousand homeless people in a grim and sunless void filled with scorpions, health risks, desperation, and addiction.

Running over three hundred miles, the intricate system of flood tunnels stretches all the way to Lake Mead, the artificial inland sea created by the construction of Hoover Dam. And since Vegas is marketed as a happy tourist town—and the homeless typically aren't good for business—the local law enforcement and city council codes have pushed Sin City's less fortunate underground, literally.

Out of sight; out of mind.

"As long as you're not bothering the tourists, the police aren't going to bother you," explained John, who was situated in the middle of the long, dark labyrinth. "If they pushed all the homeless above ground, they'd be visible to the tourists. And they don't want that."

The sad juxtaposition of the façade versus the reality is apparent. Above ground and just across the road sits an executive airfield where the wealthiest visitors land their multimillion dollar private jets. Hotels provide clean pillows, fresh towels, air conditioning, and a mini-bar. And casino buffets offer all you can eat meals, enticing gamblers to spend more time separating themselves—without the distraction of rumbling bellies—from their cash.

Although I met John prior to the campaign, he is one of the forgotten people Donald Trump promised to help. Many voters supported Trump since he championed the underdog and claimed that he cared about forgotten America: the working-class men and women struggling to get by. But instead of bringing back good jobs for low-income people, Trump is trying to take away their healthcare. Amid his many proposed budget cuts, Trump wants to eliminate the U.S. Interagency Council on Homelessness and shave billions of dollars of funding for the Department of Housing and Urban Development (HUD), which funds in excess of three thousand public-housing authorities with over one million units as well as the Section 8 rental-voucher program that serves more than two million families.

Under Trump's plan, there would be little federal help for John and the estimated half-million homeless people in America.

"Is it safer living down here than out on the streets?" I asked John.

"Yeah, it's quieter," he said. "Some of the guys I shoo away because they are just addicts and come down here to get high. They bring the heat with them."

Married with two kids, a beautiful house, and a successful business, John went home one day and told his wife, "It's all yours—and the kids. See ya!" He said he gave up boats, four-wheelers, a Ferrari, and a half-million dollar home.

During the next year, John worked on the docks at the Mandalay Bay casino until he was laid off. Then, he started doing odd jobs for businesses or helping people fix flat tires. "It's all day by day," he said.

The constant influx of tourists to Vegas provides a target of opportunity for many. "I've never seen so much stealing in all my life," John said. Some tunnel dwellers dress up like tourists to blend in and grab stacks of chips, purses, or wallets. Leave these pickpockets alone for a nanosecond and poof, it's gone. John once shared the tunnel with a luggage thief who fenced the contents for drug money.

"He'd bring it down to the tunnels, and there would be empty luggage and stuff streaming everywhere," John said. "It goes on all the time. It's pretty desperate here."

Desperation ignites danger. Someone looking for drugs might assault another member of the community, or teenager looking for a thrill might come down to the cavernous darkness to beat up a homeless guy.

But for tunnel dwellers, there was a greater, life-threatening danger. "They call it flushing the toilet," John said. "The rains pick up and wipe out everything." Powerful, dangerous, and impossible to predict, the runoff builds up at the other end of the flood tunnel and then rages like the torrent flowing through a burst dam, surging at speeds up to forty-nine miles per hour and filling up the tunnel within seconds.

"The water was just about over my head. It rushed over that concrete wall you passed when you came down," John said. "When you think it's going to rain, you have your stuff at the end of that tunnel, ready to move. It got me last year—swept everything away … Last two times I've beaten it though."

I stepped over a line of plastic bottles, which had been set up as a makeshift alarm system to provide inhabitants with a warning if kicked over by an intruder. It was claustrophobic and cramped down there; my flashlight's beam failed to detect an end to the elongated tunnel. It was weird to think that directly above me casinos were filled with happy (and maybe not so happy) gamblers and drunken bachelorette partygoers indulging in thirty dollar fruity, blue drinks.

"DON'T COME BACK HERE! GO BACK!" a disembodied voice suddenly roared from deep within the bowels of the tunnels. The hairs on my neck stood up. "WHO'S THAT?!"

My tour guide replied, "It's John."

The voice answered with a mighty echo, "WHAT DO YOU WANT?"

John tried to assure the man: "We're just coming to this grey area right here."

In a whispered tone, John said to me, "We don't want to disturb George. He doesn't like many people. He was in prison for a while and just stays here in the dark. You could give him a one hundred dollars, and the next day, he'll be asking you for money. It doesn't matter how much money you give him; he'll blow it all.

"That's the way most of these people think: today is their last day.

Whatever they have, they're going to consume it. They're not even going to save a single cigarette for tomorrow."

In another tunnel off of Tropicana Avenue, near a low-rent housing complex, garbage was spread everywhere and water dripped from the ceiling. It was damp and smelled like raw sewage. "Just cleaning up the place," said Cindy, attempting to be domestic under dire circumstances. "These two chairs are actually from the last flood, and they survived in the rushing water, holding on by their wheels."

She gave me the tour of the cavernous space. Much like the two chairs, Cindy, and her companion Rick, also held on for life. "The water came about this high," Cindy said, putting her hand at chin level.

"Has it been dripping for a while?" I asked while dodging the steady stream.

"The leak is getting worse. We used to have our bedroom right here," she said, showing me a huge puddle. "I made a path and cleared it. We had *Cindy and Rick* written on the wall."

The young couple has struggled with addiction: heavy drinking and the demon drug meth. Rick was thin and gaunt and had trouble maneuvering around. The light from a headlamp illuminated his surroundings as he dug through a duffel bag full of goods he found while dumpster-diving.

"What's in there?" I asked.

"Tons of good shit. Two skateboard decks, Christmas lights, porch screen," said Rick, pulling out treasures from the bag and handing the items to Cindy. "We collected all this stuff over the past few weeks 'cause our other stuff got washed away."

A kitchen area built by Rick was equipped with a camping stove and a plastic, hanging water system. A discarded table without legs sat on top of an abandoned nightstand. It was used for mealtimes and housing drug paraphernalia. Cindy decorated the place with artwork, mostly murals involving the hip hop duo Insane Clown Posse. "When Rick was in jail, I wrote, 'I Miss You,'" she said.

Near the table, Cindy pointed to some graffiti. "Anything that has gang signs will get the county out," she said. "If the county comes out, they're going to take everything and paint because of the tagging."

Rick and Cindy had lived in the tunnel on-and-off for the previous year and a half. Tragic events in their lives led them down there. "Rick's mom died of cancer, and she lived in a seniors' complex. It took both of us to take care of her in the end," said Cindy. "Since it was a seniors' complex, we had to move out right then and there."

Cindy reached into the duffel bag and removed another item. "This is a very good comb," she said.

In Las Vegas sketchy characters easily prey upon the vulnerable that live on the fringes of society. It happened to Rick on his previous job at a rented house. A guy offered him a fifty-fifty split of the profits for "recycling a bunch of copper, pulling the wires, stripping it for two hundred bucks." In classic Vegas fashion the employer gambled away Rick's payday. "He finally fucked the spring that snapped," Rick said, pulling out a Hello Kitty purse from his dumpster-diving finds.

"Is it better to live down here than in a homeless shelter? Wouldn't that be less dangerous?" I asked him.

"There's a curfew, and you have to check out and then wait in line each night with all your belongs," he said.

"Besides, they'd split us up," Cindy added with emotion. The state, in its infinite wisdom, would destroy the only human bonds that these two people had. Did it ever occur to the bureaucrats that this type of partnership might increase their odds of getting ahead? Whatever happened to family values?

"Where would you like to be next year at this time?" I asked as the stream of water grew louder.

"Rick's dream is to become rich enough to buy this piece of land and live down here with power and air," Cindy shared with a laugh. "It's funny as hell."

Mike worked at a gun shop in Las Vegas. The cozy neighborhood bar—known for its great hamburgers—where we met was a far cry from the netherworld from which he emerged and came out whole. As I looked at clean-cut Mike, a former Marine, it was hard to believe that he was once a chronic homeless person who lived a quarter of a mile inside a tunnel near the Rio All-Suite Hotel & Casino.

"It was a big, long empty tunnel. Then all of a sudden, bookcases and empty beds. People would have tents set up in there. It was pretty well furnished," Mike said, obviously straining to retell his tale.

An active-duty Marine for ten years and then a police officer back in his native Washington state, Mike didn't fit the normal profile of a chronic homeless person. His life began to slide when he lost his job and divorced. "I was told I was going to get kicked out of my apartment, so I grabbed what I could, put it in the car, and drove to

Vegas," he said. "It seemed like a plan with a lot of opportunity."

Once Mike arrived in Vegas, however, he was forced to sleep in his car, which eventually broke down in the MGM parking garage.

"I'd do sports betting and made some money out of it for a while," he said. "But in the end, the casinos win."

Casinos wouldn't be multi-billion dollar businesses if it were possible to win most of the time.

After being kicked off the MGM property, Mike grabbed what he could from his car, walked out of the garage, and started sleeping in the bushes along the airport fence. Then, he lost his wallet and ID.

For the next six years, Mike lived on the streets ... until he discovered the tunnels. "I was camping by the railroad tracks and saw a couple walking out of the tunnels dressed up all nice," he said. "She had a nice dress on." The well-dressed couple was off to hustle money by blending in with the tourists at the casinos. Soon, they welcomed Mike into their group inside the tunnel, where they lived in a communal arrangement.

The dream that Las Vegas sells is the antithesis of the community underneath. "Seeing what people pay for the price of a room, where I could live on for a month, people didn't feel bad for doing the hustling thing," Mike said. But despite constant hustling, "pretty much all the money went to drugs."

The group once found a sixteen hundred dollar winning sports ticket on the floor of a casino. It never crossed their minds that the winnings could be used to find a decent place to live for a few months. "That would go pretty fast," Mike said, "because they'd go on big benders with a lot of money."

What saved Mike was HELP of Southern Nevada. The program has assisted in removing hundreds of people from the tunnels.

"HELP deals with what they call the worst of the worst: people who have been homeless for many years and have mental health issues," said Matthew O'Brien from the Shine a Light Foundation, a community program that works with HELP to assist the homeless. At that time, he escorted HELP employees and social workers down into the tunnels and introduced them to homeless people in need of the services of the outreach program. "Because of the flooding, it's more dangerous than people just living on the streets."

HELP places tunnel-dwellers in a group home, which assesses their health and drug issues and provides counseling. If program participants show progress, they are set up with their own apartments. The goal is to move the homeless out of darkness and back into society.

As a grassroots activist helping the homeless, O'Brien was not surprised by Trump's proposed budget cuts of HUD and the elimination of the Interagency Council on Homelessness. "Trump certainly does not strike me as someone who would be progressive and out front when it comes to the poor and homeless," he said.

O'Brien has learned not to rely on outside funding—or be swayed by its possible influence. Even if Trump puts more budget money into building a border wall than helping the homeless, O'Brien won't let it affect his program. However, he fears that funding for local nonprofits such as HELP would suffer from cuts in federal funding and HUD vouchers. The people in the tunnels, therefore, might miss out on some of the housing opportunities they had previously enjoyed.

HUD estimates that each homeless individual costs taxpayers forty thousand dollars per year in emergency room visits, arrests, jails, and shelters. In contrast, the cost to provide supportive housing for each individual runs somewhere between thirteen thousand and twenty-five thousand dollars per year.

"In the last seven or eight years, hundreds of people have made it out of the tunnels and turned their lives around," O'Brien said. "It would be a shame to see those opportunities dry up. The folks in the tunnels don't have nearly enough options as it is."

In the meantime, it's not an easy road for a person living in the tunnels to return to normal society: not everyone qualifies for HELP. John didn't since he had been homeless for less than two years. Potential candidates must also be drug-free. "I don't think Rick and Cindy are ready at this moment," O'Brien said.

"None of us in my group wanted in the program because we didn't want to be locked down in a halfway house," Mike said. After being evaluated, he was placed in a duplex with six other HELP participants and assigned a counselor. The program assisted Mike in acquiring a state-issued ID and a Social Security card: two important documents to help him return to the norms of society. "They pay the rent and all the bills," Mike said. "The main thing is once you finish counseling you look for work."

But his transition back into society was far from smooth. The eight-year gap in his job history—while living in the tunnels for several of those years—was his biggest problem and the most difficult thing to explain to a potential employer.

As a result, things started going back downhill for Mike. "I actually went back to sports betting," he said. "It wasn't smart, but I didn't know what to do."

To earn extra money, Mike sold plasma. During one visit to the blood bank, he checked local job listings and saw that the gun store was hiring. "When he applied he was totally honest about his past and was hired on the spot," said Mike's fiancée. "A lot of employers would not be open to that."

Mike became a model employee and moved in with his fiancée in a comfortable two-bedroom apartment in the suburbs, a far cry from his former subterranean hell beneath the streets of Las Vegas. The couple told me that they occasionally hosted dinner parties at their home, inviting Mike's friends from the tunnels, who, for the most part, weren't faring as well: chronic homelessness, addiction, jail, and death.

Mike credited his strength for his survival in the tunnels and on the streets of Las Vegas. "You need perseverance when living on the streets," he said before we parted. "The important thing is just going day to day and not giving up."

CHAPTER 18

THE SMELL OF METH IN THE MORNING

Some people look at their dead-end lives and wallow in despair. Others take action: they buy drugs and get wasted. As we waded through a room filled with a sea of garbage—a mirror reflection of someone's worst moments littered all over the floor—Rick said, "They got junkies out there that are so desperate they'll come back and lick the walls." After a moment he asked, "Do you know that smell? That's what they want." I nodded my head. Of course I didn't know it.

Amongst the used syringes on the coffee table, I found a book, *Know the Word of Jesus in 30 Days*, which was probably not an impulse read. Into the trash it went.

"That high is never duplicated," Rick continued. "I know this is gross, but they will even try to get it out of their urine ... That's sick."

Some of the toothless smiles you see in rural Indiana are likely the result of meth addiction. The Hoosier State may be dotted with churches, crosses, and basketball courts, but it's also the third-largest meth capital in America—right behind Missouri and Tennessee. It is the kind of state that Trump would call—like he did New Hampshire—"a drug infested den." While governor of Indiana, Vice-President Mike Pence failed to act quickly enough to halt the spread of both the meth and opioid epidemics in his state, which in turn led to a spiraling HIV outbreak as a result of addicts sharing needles.

Trump claims that the drugs are pouring in over the Mexican border, as did Pence, who advocated using U.S. military personnel to patrol that region to stop the influx of drugs. But in Indiana's case, the drugs weren't coming nearly as far: they were being manufactured in suburban basements by mixing a few simple items purchased at the local big-box store. But rather than declaring this a health emergency, Pence broadened the "war on drugs" by supporting maximum prison sentences for addicts.

In the small town of Plainville—a depressed (and conservative) Bible Belt community, complete with dilapidated houses, welcoming churches, and large **Stop Abortion** signs—it's *Breaking Bad* for real.

"Not a half-bad day," quipped the cheery clerk at the Circle K, who was unaware that just past Main Street stood the remnants of a foul meth lab. But instead of resorting to cooking in a RV like chemistry teacher Walter White, a local family-owned business found a new meth-related vocation during these hard times.

"We do death and meth," said Donetta J. Held, who runs Crisis Cleaning, the top meth-lab cleanup company in Indiana. Since 2007, the demand for their services has dramatically risen: a sad barometer of Indiana's economic climate. Meth is the drug of choice for the poor since it can be manufactured using common household items found at Walmart.

"Evansville is number one for Indiana," said Donetta, whose family construction company was founded in 1955 to deal with fire and water damage. Three generations later, the biggest type of cleanup they do is meth. "We'll go through periods where we get daily phone calls."

Exactly how did the family business transition into this new area of expertise? "At trade shows, police started asking us, 'Do you do meth lab cleaning?' They were asking for help!" said Donetta from the front of a low-rent brick apartment complex on the edge of town. "When I was a little girl working for my dad's construction business, I never thought I'd end up in death and meth."

Ain't adulthood grand?

As her husband Rick suited up with his team in matching blue jumpsuits, he piped in with a smirk, "I married into this."

This may come as a total shock, but cleaning meth labs isn't as glamorous as one would imagine. If certain volatile chemicals are inhaled without a mask, they can melt your lungs. Kidney ailments and respiratory problems could also occur.

Sometimes meth cooks boobytrap their houses by filling light bulbs with gasoline. If the police bust in and flip a switch, the ambushed light fixture explodes.

"Assume everything is booby-trapped. You never know what you'll find!" warned Donetta.

"Bill was here last week with his respirator mask on, and he felt it," said Rick as he handed me a pair of white booties, gloves, and a ventilator.

"What did you feel?" I asked Bill while snugly fitting my mask into place.

"You get a sore throat pretty quick. It starts bothering your sinuses," Bill dryly explained. "Even if you're in there for a only a few minutes, it bothers you for a few hours."

Rick elaborated: "It gets into your pores and you start itching your arms. That's where they start getting the scabs and missing teeth. If you went in there without the right equipment, you'd be sick for a couple of days ... But it's a fun job!"

It was so much fun you that the excitement could literally kill you.

The crew looked as though it were about to enter a Chernobyl reactor hours after meltdown. "Let's go in!" I proclaimed. Then, we stepped over a large patch of dead grass, through the front door, and into a manic guy's crazed head during his spiral descent into the abyss: a sad legacy left behind in a cockroach-infested pit.

"It's almost like the TV reality show *Hoarders*. You just don't know what you're going to find," said Rick as we sifted through trash. "I once kicked a guy. He was lying on floor coming down from meth, and I didn't see him."

The lab in this small apartment had been busted by the cops two months earlier, and it would take about three days to cleanup, which was a fast turnaround. Due to red tape, it can take up to a year before some homes are cleaned.

The majority of meth labs occur in rental properties. Since meth is considered a pollutant (or an act of vandalism), cleanup is typically covered by insurance. Landlords are paid for lost rent, with the busted tenants bearing none of the financial responsibility. But insurance companies are starting to catch on by inserting methamphetamine exclusions in policies.

"We're testing places from the winter because that's when they cook inside," said Rick, rummaging through the junkie's belongs as though he were at a gloomy garage sale. "Now that it's summer, they cook outside."

The deserted apartment told a twisted story through the discarded remnants of a sad, distant past: a family photo album, foster parent papers, a closet with shoes stacked a foot high, and an American flag draped across the bed.

Rick picked up a handful of bullets, which were scattered all over the floor. "They're paranoid. They think everybody's after them," he said. "I've been in homes where they literally had guns everywhere. It's incredible!"

Heavily armed, paranoid, and cranked on meth: it's the great American Dream.

"It's interesting what you go through," Rick said while tearing out the bathroom exhaust. "The last place we cleaned, they left the urn of their deceased father. They do odd things—definitely odd things."

As I threw a completion certificate from an anger-management course into a garbage bag, I asked, "What kind of things?"

Rick replied, "Just weird things they get into because they're on meth. Their brains are like Einstein's. They'll get crazy smart."

He pulled out a box of ripped-apart wires and electronic components and pointed to the set of hand tools scattered on the bed. "Notice the tools. Their brains are working so hard," he said. "They'll take apart a DVD player and put it back together again. And then ask, 'Why did I do that?'"

With strange admiration for his archnemesis meth cooks, Rick added, "The police are two steps behind them because their brains are going so fast."

As the chemicals started to make their way inside my nose and eyes, a thin layer coated my teeth like meth sandpaper, leaving a metallic taste that lingered in my mouth.

"The police found some meth here," said Rick, acknowledging a large hole in the living room wall. "The American flag was over the hole. That's where he kept his drugs."

The blue-suited workers continued stuffing garbage—used

aluminum foil, empty Mountain Dew bottles (for shake and bake), pills, etc.—into large, black bin bags. Rick came across several glass tubes and a snorkel mouthpiece that had been converted into meth pipes. "This is how they smoked it," he said.

From under the couch, he pulled out a wad of aluminum foil dotted with a large blob of grey ash and said, "Here's your meth."

While looking around at the sea of shit that was this man's life, Rick summarized: "They're high—the highest high ever. They'll never be that high again, and they're locked into it."

At this property, the clues were as subtle as a rocket launch. Near the shed, the backyard was covered with circles of dead, yellow grass and piles of syringes. A large propane tank sat next to a bucket with a hole in the bottom that had been burnt through from pouring out test cooks.

"The average person buying property doesn't think to look for these signs," Donetta said, which included big burn piles in the backyard, dead grass where chemicals had been dumped, and chemical stains in tubs and sinks.

"How realistic is *Breaking Bad*?" I asked Donetta while removing my ventilator mask and breathing in precious fresh air—life's juices.

"I'd say fifty-fifty," she said. "The technical process and making it, they got right." Interestingly, the show's producers told interviewers that they intentionally edited the cook process in order to baffle would-be copycats.

"Have you ever come across someone cooking in a Winnebago?" I asked.

After a moment's thought, Donetta replied, "We've done trailer parks. Everyone has a picture of a meth home looking like this."

Conversely, the range of meth labs runs from beautiful cathedral homes to the slum we were cleaning. Why couldn't I have seen a ruined McMansion? "People have bought property, and after the purchase, they found out that a meth lab was there," she added. Imagine the shock when the police break this news to a homeowner.

Twenty years after being used to cook meth, a house could still be contaminated, even though the place has been aired out and slapped with a fresh coat of paint, which doesn't get rid of the fumes left behind. Thank you, Century 21!

Police dogs can't even detect meth residue that lingers on walls and carpets. As a result, health problems arise. Residents get headaches, small children develop skin rashes, and respiratory problems occur.

"I would be scared to buy property in Green County without testing it first," Donetta laughed. "I'd say fifty percent of the homes are former meth labs."

While a crusty couch was being removed from the apartment, I asked her, "Why is Indiana so popular for meth?"

She replied, "It's rural."

Since meth is so easy to manufacture, meth addicts, like *Night of the Living Dead* zombies, sneak onto farms and steal barrels of hydrous ammonia—a main ingredient in the meth recipe.

"It's ... easy to make. You don't have to buy your drugs from anybody," Donetta informed me. "If you want it, you can just go buy or steal the ingredients."

To circumvent a 2005 federal law that bars customers from purchasing more than nine grams—approximately three hundred pills—of pseudoephedrine per month, a majority (seventy-five percent) of individual-use meth labs in Indiana have resorted to the shake and bake method, the lowest level of meth production.

With shake and bake (also known as the one pot method), tweakers acquire from Walmart a single package of Sudafed, whose main ingredient is pseudoephedrine. To cook the meth, all the components are mixed together in a two-liter plastic soda bottle. When shaken up, the meth crystallizes instantly. The chemicals, however, are extremely volatile and can explode like a bomb.

"These guys aren't chemists. They're not doing it right," Donetta said. "They'll make it in their cars, but they need more room. Remember, they got to drain the chemicals."

Rick, who was taking a break, added: "A guy was doing shake and bake in his car. It blew up, and the windshield shot back and killed him."

A late model car drove by and slowed down, making me nervous. At the apartment complex, several front doors were open, allowing residents to witness the men in blue biohazard jumpsuits carrying garbage from the building and placing it into a large, metal trash trailer.

"Maybelle! Maybelle!" screamed a neighbor, Carol, from behind a screen door. Her dog lunged at me, and I maneuvered towards her. "Did you know the man next door?" I asked her.

"He was a really nice guy," answered Carol, a heavyset woman with hard life tales etched on her face. She was keen to talk to me. "But he started weirding out when he and his girlfriend broke up."

When he moved in, the first thing he told Carol was that he had suffered six nervous breakdowns. "He was ... *different*," she added.

After he started cooking, strange things were afoot. He stopped being social and kept to himself. "You'd hear water running all night. When he answered the door, he always had rubber gloves on," she explained. "I thought that was weird. The people over here would talk to him a lot because he'd make them cigarettes." He was always cutting up batteries, she added.

Carol was forced to reside in the low-rent apartment complex—with her mom and sister—as a result of a disability: she was shot in the leg during a gunfight that killed her boyfriend.

The previous Christmas, the stench of meth was so strong that Carol could smell it through the walls of her apartment. As a result, she developed terrible headaches. Other residents started complaining.

"The first few times, the police told me they're too busy. Finally, these people here went to town and talked to a cop they knew," she said. "When the police went to see him, the smell was so strong that the cop was just wiping his eyes."

As Carol picked up Maybelle, who had now returned home, she added: "I'm glad he's in jail because my headaches have gone down."

When a man is on the verge of losing everything, what does he attach to his refrigerator with a magnet? A pest control company's phone number, a photo of his elderly parents, and a subscription card for *Ski Magazine*. It seemed as if he were trying to say, "When I get it together, I'm going to take my parents skiing while my place is being exterminated."

In a house littered with shit, the kitchen is always the worst: broken dishes, empty rum bottles, cigarette butts, caked saucepans, paranoia, suspicion, and a manic mind in overtime.

When police raid a lab and confiscate the equipment, the Health Department is notified and the property has to be decontaminated by a state-certified company like Crisis Cleaning. To be habitable, a room must test at a level below 0.5 micrograms of meth residue per hundred square centimeters. This kitchen clocked in at 9.73.

"They cooked it here and poured it down the drain," Rick said authoritatively as we waddled through a mound of discarded blue rubber gloves. "That's why the kitchen is the hottest. Every time he cooked, it was a new pair of gloves." After assessing the quantity of discarded gloves, Rick concluded that they had been cooking for "over eight months."

He picked up an AA Energizer from a pile of batteries at our feet. "They're putting Lithium into the meth," he said. A cupboard housed a tub of batteries, and disassembled cell phones—with batteries pulled out—lay in mass on the counter. "This is just strictly for him. He's an addict, and it's for personal use. They want that high back ... I guess it's an incredible high!"

I had a headache, nausea, and sandpaper meth grit on my teeth, which made me want to pull them out. Lunch at Pizza Hut didn't help matters either.

The living room was now a bare shell. Meth fumes had caused streaking in the paint. Once the carpet was ripped out—and all the syringes and other dangerous drug paraphernalia had been removed— the actual cleaning process began. The air duct system was fogged, and Chrystal Clean, a foam disinfectant developed by the government to kill anthrax (you know, as in anthrax), was sprayed on the walls, ceilings, and floors. The chemicals bubbled up and neutralized the toxins. After the foam sat for an hour, we simply rinsed it off with a cleaning agent and water.

"It gets all of the contaminants out the first time," Donetta said. Finally, every square inch was vacuumed up. The room was humidified and left to dry, and we were done. No fuss! No muss! No more meth!

For the home to be certified, state law requires that meth residue levels are tested by taking four alcohol swabs from each room.

"I'm going to go here in the center by the door and by the ceiling," said Bill. The swabs are then put into a vial and sent overnight to a lab in Washington state. The results are returned in three to five days.

"What is the typical meth user?" I asked the couple while standing in the middle of the empty space.

"A white person," Donetta said. "Any white person out there could be addicted to meth. There is no one stereotype." (Other than "a white person.")

"But there are good people out there, and they're not thinking. Eighty percent of them do it and get addicted," Rick said over a humidifier blast. "Part is—they're depressed at what's going on with life. I feel sorry for them. I really do. But there's other ways to deal with it ... You're just screwing the whole purpose of life."

The empty room went silent except for the hum of the humidifier and the barking of Maybelle from across the dead patches of yellow grass.

CHAPTER 19

KNIGHTS IN SHINING WHITE JUMPSUITS

WHEN A PERSON IS shot in the head and their cerebellum splatters against a bedroom wall, the brains are very hard to clean off the surface. Popcorn ceilings are the worst: matter gets stuck between the crevices. Brains are comprised of twelve percent fat—essentially they're cholesterol, which hardens when it dries. The brains I was cleaning had been on the wall for only a few hours. I tried to imagine the difficulty of the task if the substance had been lingering for weeks.

"You have to hydrate it," David O'Brian explained to me and his other attentive pupils, who were dressed in matching white jumpsuits. "Soaking it in CVC re-hydrates it."

For the last eight years Dave has been a crime scene cleaner, decontaminating toxic scenes of grisly murders, suicides, meth labs, and hoarder homes. He previously worked as a body transporter at a crematorium. After hearing someone describe a death scene, he told his wife, "Honey, this is something I could do." Now, in addition to the job, he also conducts a hands-on training academy for those who want to learn the fine points of being a Trauma Scene Medical Waste Practitioner.

"Someone's got to do it," Dave said in an off-handed manner. But while I was with him, Dave took his work seriously. For instance, he is not a fan of the wacky 2008 comedy film, *Sunshine Cleaning*, about his profession. "That movie is a joke," he scoffed. "They pull a mattress out of a crime scene and keep tripping over it."

In real life a bloody mattress is a biohazard. A professional cleaner dons protective gear and cuts up the contaminated material into eight-to-ten inch squares, layering them in a red biohazard bag. "I treat everything like it's potentially infectious," Dave stressed. "This is not a joke."

Crime-scene cleaning is a burgeoning industry in this age of American carnage, echoed by Trump's dark vision of America. The president claims that the murder rate is higher than it has been in forty-seven years. This theme was a consistent force during his campaign, despite the fact that the national homicide rate is considerably lower today than at its peak in the 1990s. But his fabricated rhetoric did the trick of scaring the beejeebees out of his followers.

A few of Trump's supporters, who are looking to change their employment circumstances, have turned towards the cleaning and disposal of American carnage. According to Dave, this industry contains very few skilled workers. "Usually they have a carpet cleaning company do the work," he said. "But they are not trained." Dave's training costs five thousand dollars, but often, one job can pay for it.

For example, Dave undertook a forty thousand dollar gig after an unnamed Hollywood starlet passed away. He said that the flies from the deceased woman's premise had infested the bathroom of the downstairs condo and transmitted contamination by landing on the inhabitants' toothbrushes. As a result, that condo also required decontamination.

Then there was the twenty-eight thousand dollar job in a house inhabited by an elderly lady and her dozens of cats. When her body was found, the felines had begun to eat her. Me-ow! "It took two weeks to clean up. For six years, those cats were using the whole house as a toilet," he recalled. "You know, I love these jobs where there's shit up to my knees. They pay the best, and it usually takes only fifteen minutes to clean up."

Eight of us were gathered in the gated community of a Las Vegas suburb for Dave's crime scene-cleaning class. The backyard of the house Dave rented for the simulated cleanup—from a woman whose mother was sick and needed the extra money to pay medical bills—literally smelled of death. His crew had splattered the bedrooms with animal blood and littered them with live maggots.

If it weren't for the lack of economic opportunities, and seeing blood and guts as a golden beacon, it was doubtful that many of these wannabe knights would have been there training to clean up splattered brain matter. A man from a mainstream cleaning operation in Kansas City told me that he and his work partner chose to expand their services when their business began to slow down. After his company was asked to clean up the remains of a man gunned down at a bus stop, the idea for a new vocation choice was born.

"We didn't know how to do that," he said. "That's why we came out here. It's a really good time to get into this business."

Tim, a decontamination specialist from New England, grinned and said, "Wait until you get to that famous pillow! Amber's in there playing with the maggots." Amber, the owner of a crime-scene cleaning outfit in Virginia, was there with some relatives to receive advanced training from Dave. But all I could think about were the possible horrors that had been concocted for us in the "famous pillow."

We suited up outside by the garage and were now ready to take on the faux crime scene. I zipped up my white jumpsuit, size XXL, which added mobility and prevented the crotch from ripping while wiping up spilled brain matter. Next, wrists were duct-taped to the sleeves, and respirators were tested. Finally, each of us put on a triple pair of gloves—that way, if a cellphone rang, the top glove easily could be removed for cleanliness. Our seven-person crew looked like a merry band of sweating Stay Puft Marshmallow men and women. To avoid overheating, we spent twenty minutes working followed by a ten-minute break—just as we would have on a real job.

"How do you mentally prepare for a real-life crime scene job?" I asked Amber as she emerged from behind closed doors.

"Maggots do a number on me. I just pretend they are caterpillars," she said with a charming Southern smile. "Nothing can really mentally prepare you for the real thing. When you enter a crime scene, be sure to know where the body is so you know where the blood has sprayed."

According to Amber, there were rewards. "You're going to feel like you know these people because you're cleaning their stuff. They'll thank you with tears in their eyes," she said, regarding cleaning up a family's house after a murder or suicide.

"You have to detach," Dave added. "They'll want to talk. Don't have long conversations. Don't tell them anything personal. You're there to work!"

Mentally prepared or not, there was no disguising what the work entailed. "When a body expands and blows up, you get all the gases, the hair, the matter—everywhere," Dave explained. "You pull up to the house and flies are already all over your car."

Amber told me about a job she once did that "had urine bottles everywhere. The tub and toilet were filled with defecation. It was hard as a rock from sitting there for so many weeks," she said. "That stuff is disgusting."

Tim added, "You find crazy stuff on suicide cleanups." That aside reminded Dave to advise the class not to wear perfume or cologne on the job in order to avoid families from associating the scent "with their fourteen-year-old son who blew his head off."

Finally, we entered the contaminated house and moved from the cold zone to the hot zone: the biohazard bedrooms. A strong stench of blood wafted through the suburban home. Deploying gallows humor, Dave proclaimed, "I smell money!"

Like a colony of white Smurfs, we tromped through the blood-splattered place. "Viv, the smell should only last for about two days," Dave assured the homeowner.

Viv took a whiff of the horrendous odor that was permeating her home. With forced optimism and a weak smile, she lied, "It's not so bad."

Dave swung open the door to the first bedroom, which looked like the location of a recent Manson Family reunion. Fake brains—comprised of chicken fat—had been splattered thickly over the walls, and in an elaborate Jackson Pollock-style, animal blood was sprayed everywhere. The beds were soaked in a dry, dark red residue, and maggots squirmed on the floor. The stench—murky and thick—went straight to my watering eyes.

"Always be aware of your surroundings," Dave commanded. "This is what it smells like after a few hours. Imagine what it smells like after a few weeks. The smell will get up in your mucus membranes and stay there for two weeks.

"If anyone feels the least bit woozy, stop. I want you to take a break.

No matter how gruesome this is, nothing will prepare you for the real thing."

Dave then gestured to a box in the corner. "Unhook that bag. Hold that container up," he said as we uncomfortably shifted from foot to foot while waiting for the unwrapping of the Christmas surprise. It was, of course, the "infamous pillow"—or rather its brown, crusty remnants, which were taken from beneath the cranium of a deceased prostitute at an actual crime scene.

"I want you to get familiar with the smell," Dave said as we lined up to take a whiff. "It's the smell of death, and you should know how to identify it."

The group teamed up to clean the two blood- and brain-stained bedrooms and one blood-covered bathroom. "Cut up the mattress with a utility knife," Dave ordered. "Wherever you see blood, cut it out."

The CVC chemical spray—which kills every germ known to humanity—made me sneeze inside my respirator mask.

"What makes me sick is warm water mixed with blood, toilet paper, and Clorox," Dave confessed.

One of Amber's relatives was red in the face and looked physically distraught while spraying the bloody walls with CVC. He made light circular motions with a paper towel, the best technique to remove body fluid. Meanwhile, his cheery wife took a load of matter to the nearby red biohazard bags.

"Whoops! I dropped some brains," she said with a smile.

"I have every single photo of every single scene. One-hundred eighty photos per scene," Dave said as I waded through maggots. The stench of blood now enveloped my every pore and stuck to my hair. "This is a good job—for the right people."

But he was not satisfied with the quality of our work. "There's blood right there," he said, pointing out missed details in the bathroom. As more brain matter was removed, he added, "There's nothing glamorous about this. We're not looking for fame. We're here to help the distraught. At their worst moment, we're their knights in shining armor."

CHAPTER 20

SHOUT AT THE DEVIL

THE SIGN OUTSIDE THE building read: *Every Saint Has A Past, Every Hellion A Future.* This had to be the place. Pulling into the parking lot, I was pretty positive at some point I would hear the devil referred to as a "douchebag."

I parked next to a stack of motorcycles, pick-up trucks, and an old school bus with a German iron cross and the words **FIRST HEAVY METAL CHURCH OF CHRIST**—in the Iron Maiden album cover font—painted on the side.

"Woo!" said the enthusiastic man greeting me at the door. "Welcome to the Heavy Metal Church, bro!" He put up his hand to give me a fist-bump.

"Woo!" I offered in response, promptly returning his fist-bump proposition. I hoped to blend in by wearing, as always, a clever disguise: a sweater with a large skull on the front and a rocker headband. As it turned out, I nailed it.

I was surrounded by a sea of tattooed bikers at the First Heavy Metal

Church of Christ (FHMCC) in the Rust Belt city Dayton, Ohio—the epicenter of our nation's spiraling opioid epidemic that was once the pulsating heart of America's industrial strength—ready to put the Jesus pedal to the heavy metal.

The name of the church is a bit of a misnomer. Although it sounds like something concocted by a pious Beavis and Butthead (untrue, they're animated characters) with Ronnie James Dio (he died in 2010) hailing as the pastor, the church is not a place where the congregation worships heavy metal. Instead, it's a place where metalheads and rockers can worship Jesus Christ in an über-masculine way (as opposed to the usual *effete* Christianity with which most people are familiar).

FHMCC was founded in 2012 by Pastor Brian Smith, a heavy metal musician who became disillusioned with the Christianity of his youth. "I used to go to a church where every Sunday I was told I was going to Hell for wearing shorts or going swimming in co-ed swimming holes ... or listening to any other music than hymns," he remembered.

He left his church, armed with a cheap PA system and a stack of discount Bibles, and started his weekly FHMCC services across the street from a strip club in the backroom of a venue where his secular metal band played. After all, a religion doesn't survive for two millennia unless it's adaptable—which means letting go of tradition and accommodating indigenous culture.

"Go to all corners of the Earth and baptize all men in the name of the Holy Spirit," quoted Pastor Brian. "What better place to do that than a bar?"

As the popularity of his metal church grew, Pastor Brian moved the service to a biker bar called Jackass Flats, which soon became a standing-room-only affair. The prayer meeting attendance eventually grew big enough to hold regular Sunday services in both Dayton and its western neighbor, Greenville, Ohio (near the Indiana border), where the service, complete with a different metal band performing every week, was held inside the auditorium of a former elementary school.

As expected, the First Heavy Metal Church of Christ rocked for Jesus. However, according to Pastor Brian, the name has a double-meaning: it also refers to the "full metal of God," as denoted in the scriptures. (When I searched for "full metal of God" in the Bible, I couldn't find the phrase.)

And unlike those uptight Christian churches where parishioners are judged for showing their bare shoulders, the First Heavy Metal Church of Christ, according to its website, opens its house-of-the-holy to all:

Prostitutes, drug addicts, bikers, gang members, metalheads, felons. It doesn't matter what you've done, or where you come from. Here at the FHMCC, everyone is welcome with open arms.

Pastor Brian explained, "This is a church for people who might not feel comfortable in a traditional church setting." Therefore, he aims to provide a spiritual safe haven for tattooed and pierced Christians and the freaky folks who want a healthy dose of Jesus. "Most people want God in their lives, but think they must clean up first before coming to Christ. You don't clean up before you jump in the shower, do you? God wants you EXACTLY the way you are at this very moment."

That hooked me. Either this was going to be awesome, or this was going to be THE MOST AWESOME THING EVER! Who doesn't like head-banging—and then having their soul saved!? So as Mötely Crüe sang, let's "Shout, Shout, Shout … Shout at the devil!"

The FHMCC service began at noon, a little later than most church services. It was hard to tell exactly how many parishioners arrived hungover, but I could count at least one. (It was me.) After fist-bumping another biker, I was handed a FHMCC program with a depiction on the front of Jesus riding a Harley.

"This is truly a cross-section of what the body of Christ should look like," said Pastor Brian, referring to the crowd. "We welcome suits and ties, but concert T-shirts are encouraged. It's really not about what you wear."

There were roughly three hundred people packed inside the auditorium: bikers, their girlfriends, and regular folks, too, with little kids. Many of the worshipers were wearing black FHMCC T-shirts, which were being sold at a merchandise table near the back. If you squinted, the long-haired, bearded bikers did look sort of like biblical characters.

I took my place next to a guy with full sleeve tattoos on both arms. "Are you a musician?" he asked. I told him I played in a Christian metal band called Pray-er (rhymes with Slayer). This was, of course, total bullshit, but it gave me a stupid enough, yet credible, cover for being there. And it allowed me to get indignant about the pronunciation of my fictitious band: "It's not Prayer; it's Pray-er!"

Standing under a large FHMCC banner (also in the same Iron Maiden font), Pastor Ron, a bearded guy who if cast in a motorcycle movie would probably be nicknamed "Tiny," proclaimed: "We're going to have healing, redemption, salvation, and deliverance take place here today."

The crowd went, "Woo!"

Then we rocked.

"Get your hands clapping! Come on!" said the guitarist, adorned in black and playing Judas Priest-style guitar with his four-piece combo.

"Woo!" again went the crowd as they threw their hands up in the air.

It was a head-thrashing, blood-pumping tune with decidedly Jesus-y lyrics: "I believe / How about you? / I believe / It's true / I believe in HIM!"

Jesus probably was the first metalhead. If nothing else, then he was certainly the first to rock long hair. And if his time on the cross showed anything, he was into piercing and body modification. Oh, and he also turned water into wine. That dude knew how to party.

"WE SAY HOLY, HOLY, HOLY!"

Rock on, Christ. Rock on!

When the opening act ended, Pastor Brian took to the black pulpit, which was adorned with a large, red-colored heavy metal cross. The self-proclaimed "Rebel for Christ" made an Angus Young allusion in reference to the church's guitarist and mentioned that FHMCC was forming a house band in need of a drummer.

Whether in the land of the secular or the house of God, the drummer is always the hardest spot in a band to fill.

"Last Sunday, four confirmed people came to Jesus for the very first time in their lives," Pastor Brian announced. "We've had three hundred baptisms in seven months. There are churches that don't get three hundred baptisms in a decade. Isn't that amazing? God rocks!"

Everyone screamed, "Woooooo!" I "wooed" with them and accidentally made devil horns with my fingers.

"God is using this church in amazing ways," Pastor Brian declared. "And it's plain just ticking the devil off!"

Once again: "Woo!"

And then we rocked again: more metal and more head-swaying. If gospel music is a mainstay of Southern Baptist churches, then heavy metal plays the same role here in blue-collar Ohio.

When the music finally concluded, Pastor Brian delivered a classic rock sermon: "Pink Floyd's *The Wall* came to me when I read the book of Philemon. It's like, tear down the wall."

Silence overcame the room. He continued, "That is the theme song of the book of Philemon—tearing down the wall."

Pastor Brian then explained that both Pink Floyd and Jesus Christ, unlike Trump, were the great wall-removers. Awesome! Rock on!

Pastor Brian believes that, if led by the right pastor, there could be a First Heavy Metal Church of Christ in every major city. Perhaps not surprisingly, he has found that the church's main opposition is other Christian groups, and they communicate via angry hate mail: "You need to quit the First Church of Satan. You're leading your congregation to the pits of Hell. Repent!"

Yet he has remained steadfast. "A lot of people, when they hear the name alone, automatically judge us," Pastor Brian said. "We've been called a cult. I've heard everything from we 'serve beer at our services' to we're nothing but a 'bunch of hell-raisers that want to live the way they want and play church on Sunday.'"

He paused. "Nothing is further from the truth. The devil is alive and well, and he'll use Christians and non-Christians to do his bidding."

Prompted by this unexpected hate from rival Christians, Pastor Brian penned a pamphlet called "Christians That Give Jesus A Bad Name," which he passes out at secular metal shows in order to connect with people who have had a bad experience with church. The catalyst was a 2006 Marilyn Manson concert where he saw a group of "super-Christians" carrying signs and yelling through bullhorns at the kids walking in, not so subtly informing them that they were going to burn in Hell.

"The kids were yelling obscenities back. It was just horrible," Pastor Brian recalled. "They were just doing it all wrong. If you want to win kids over to Christ, you attract more bees with honey and not vinegar. I'd rather love the hell out of you than scare the hell out of you."

Pastor Brian concluded that this wasn't the way Jesus would have done it: "Let's get together and save these lost souls because the world is going to hell in a bucket right before our eyes. The devil is the real enemy." He added: "That's what I've learned from this ministry. I can forgive sinners all day long—sinners and saints alike. We have to forgive them."

Pastor Brian's secular metal band was less forgiving, though. They recently parted ways after complaining that Brian was way too often pushing FHMCC during mainstream gigs.

Pastor Brian concluded the heavy metal service by sharing an anecdote about Led Zeppelin singer Robert Plant: "I was up at five in the morning working on my sermon, and I thought, 'I hope Robert Plant makes it up to heaven.'"

Heavy metal laughs echoed throughout.

"Robert, I hope you make it to heaven, and we can be singing together on the streets of gold," he continued. "Then it dawned on me. What about that homeless man on the corner? I put Robert Plant on a pedestal ... because he is one of my vocal heroes. But I want that same kind of passion for everyone out there, even people who hurt me and spit on me. We need that passion for all lost people, for all people."

Amens roared from the crowd.

"This is where I'm going to leave you today," said Pastor Brian. "If you want easy, go live like a rock star. Being a Christian, it's not easy—it's not. But I'm telling you, it's worth it."

Once again, we ROCKED! Not only did we rock, but we also hugged big bikers as they prayed for us at the front of the auditorium. (It felt so secure and comforting—and totally hetero—to be held in their big arms.) As the music built, a few big, tough bikers, with their heads and hands lifted upwards, began to cry. Looking around at people conservative Christians would call "misfits," I thought that if I had to believe in an infinite and invisible magic man in the sky, then this would be my go-to place.

While waiting in line for a word with Brian, I started talking to a large guy who was wearing a motorcycle patch that said **Satan Sucks**. Before complimenting my skull sweater, he informed me that he was the lead singer of a mainstream punk band that played Dead Kennedy and Clutch covers. I told him about my fictional Christian band, Prayer. ("Prayer?" "No, Pray-er.")

"I used to do shows and all I could think about was getting the show over so I could go meet my drug dealer," he said about life before FHMCC. "Then I met Brian at a metal show. When I first met him, I had a beer in each hand—and he still invited me to his church."

Fulfilling my prophecy, I agreed, "The devil's a real douchebag."

Even though Mr. Satan Sucks still played in his punk band, he was now sober. He credited the FHMCC for saving his life.

"Have you changed your set list at all now that you've found Jesus?" I asked.

"I won't do the Rage Against the Machine song 'Killing in the Name,'" he said. "It has all that swearing at the end."

If, and when, I ever experience a bad case of heatstroke and have a Paul-on-the-road-to-Damascus-like moment, then Dayton, Ohio will probably be the first stop on my road to redemption.

AFTERWORD

THANKS TO TRUMP, A NEW LEFT RISES

ALL THE MEDIA PEOPLE who keep repeating that "nobody" saw Donald Trump's "upset" win coming are seriously annoying. I saw it coming a million miles away. Let me pinch myself to find out if I am someone who is *here*. Yep, I still exist. Is it really possible that I'm the only pundit in America who grew up in the Rust Belt and still goes home to visit?

Of course the corporate media morons didn't see this mess coming. They missed the housing bubble, and then they missed, or ignored, the fact that the bursting of said bubble would have dire long-term consequences, not the least of which was the result of the 2016 election.

During the primaries, the corporate media didn't take Donald Trump seriously (c.f., Ross Douthat, *New York Times*, March 8, 2016: "Donald Trump will not be the Republican nominee"). Then, when it was clear that Trump would win the GOP nomination, they ignored polls that repeatedly showed Bernie Sanders to be a better candidate than Hillary Clinton against Donald Trump. It certainly never occurred to them that reducing tens of millions of middle-class workers to poverty—in order to line the pockets of globalization-besotted elites—might turn said impoverished citizens into tens of millions of angry voters.

Furthermore, Democrats, following the debacle, never internalized that what went wrong was them—that their mistaken assessments of nearly everything helped move the needle toward Trumpism. They took no responsibility and blamed everyone else: WikiLeaks, Russia, the FBI, the media, even Bernie voters. They didn't think they did anything wrong.

But it's not all bad news.

There's something else that neither the corporate media nor the Democrats see coming: the rise of a new American Left—one whose size and militancy recalls the glory days of the 1960s and is energized and united by its opposition to Donald Trump and his policies.

There's something happening here.

Well, there soon will be.

As I wrote in my 2010 book *The Anti-American Manifesto*, the United States does not have a Left in the way other nations think of the term—an organization or movement dedicated to the radical overthrow of the existing political and economic order. As Chris Hedges has eloquently described, this country has even lost its bourgeois twentieth century liberal class.

In most developed countries Leftists and liberals are part of the mainstream political conversation. Here, however, a tacit ongoing conspiracy between media gatekeepers and corporate Democratic and Republican political leaders has marginalized the roughly thirty-five percent of Americans who oppose capitalism and militarism. Think about it: when was the last time you saw someone completely opposed to military action speaking on cable television news? Recall communists or socialists hired to write for a newspaper or magazine?

The silencing of the American Left, brutal and relentless since the early 1970s, has impoverished our political culture and deprived the poor and oppressed of the help to which they are entitled by birthright. But that's about to come to an end.

The future of the Democrats lies with progressives, and there is a real chance for a genuine left-of-center Democratic Party presidential candidate, with coattails, capable of defeating the Republicans in 2020.

Trumpism is making us question everything, including longstanding shibboleths. There are calls for new Constitutional conventions, including amending or repealing the Second Amendment's perceived universal right to bear arms. Even more than in the aftermath of the election of George W. Bush, Donald Trump's Electoral College win/popular vote loss has provided new impetus for eliminating the antiquated Electoral College system once and for all.

The two-party system has survived two centuries, but it is in serious trouble because of Trump—and that's a good thing. We're a big country. We deserve more than two viable political parties to represent us and our dreams and aspirations.

Trumpism is fracturing the GOP, not merely via the widely reported schism between the Tea Party right—including the House Freedom Caucus—and the corporate "establishment" Bush-type Republicans but between the true believers and the sane.

Outgoing GOP Senator Bob Corker, a Tennessean not known for his liberalism, convened hearings to consider whether President Trump can be trusted with the exclusive power to launch nuclear weapons. Yes, the question of whether one person should have the ability to destroy the planet is important.

But the discussion Corker initiated prompts another question: why now? Because in the nuclear age this president makes people worry more about that power than previous leaders.

Members of the House of Representatives are attempting to gather support for Articles of Impeachment to be filed against the president. Some say they expect Republicans to sign on to the effort as soon as Trump's approval rating among Republican voters falls further. "Privately they will tell you, by their words and by their expressions, that they would like to see an end to the Trump administration and don't approve of what he's doing," Representative Steve Cohen (D-TN) told *Newsweek* in October 2017.

Meanwhile, out in the streets where real political change can happen, I expect to see an anti-Trump resistance movement (that incorporates anarchists, veterans of the Occupy Wall Street movement, communists and socialists, radicalized left-wing Democrats, old 1960s hippies, Black Lives Matter activists, and pro-immigrant supporters) working together and individually to oppose the radical right policies that will be flying out of Washington over the next few years.

We've already seen the inspiring Women's March of January 21,

2017 (though much of the resulting energy from that event appears to have been directed more toward electing Democratic politicians than street action).

As Trumpism increasingly turns inward (think Nixon between Watergate and his resignation), simultaneously exposing itself as inane, inept, and corrupt, it will radicalize rightward, inevitably precipitating an equal, opposite radicalization on the political left.

Out on the streets, Trump's repressive tone will prompt brutal police tactics to which nonviolence will no longer be seen as the only acceptable counteraction. The "peace police" of the wimpy protests of the 1990s and 2000s will go extinct. Refuse Fascism, one of the leading organizers of anti-Trump street protests, calls for nonviolence but invites everyone who opposes the president's regime to join them, asserting that protesters are entitled to defend themselves against right-wing counterprotesters and over-zealous police if they so choose. This is as it should be: nonviolence will retake its rightful place as a noble and desirable tactic but no longer the exclusive approach to taking on a repressive government and freelance goons.

As long as Trump and Trumpism last, both will be atrocious for the United States. Trump will continue to attack immigrants, Latinos, Muslims, victims of police brutality ... and God knows who else.

But he'll be good for the Left. And, in the long run, the Left will truly *Make America Great Again*—for the first time.

–**Ted Rall**

ACKNOWLEDGMENTS

HARMON LEON is grateful to the editors of the following books and periodicals where his infiltrations first appeared:

BOOKS

The Infiltrator: My Undercover Exploits in Right-Wing America (Prometheus Books, 2006): "Angry Villagers Chasing Aliens"

Republican Like Me: Infiltrating Red-State, White-Ass, and Blue-Suit America (Prometheus Books, 2005): "Unborn Jesus & the Grim Reaper," "Hit Me with Your Best Ex-gay Shot"

PERIODICALS

Cracked: "Janie Got a Gun ... on Facebook," "Not on Our Watch"

Maxim: "The Smell of Meth in the Morning"

Ozy: "Knocking on Doors for Trump"

Penthouse: "Here Comes the Repo Man," "Knights in Shiny White Jumpsuits"

Vice: "Best Little Hell House in Texas," "Fear & Loathing Beneath Las Vegas," "He Blinded Me with Biblical Science," "Ink Me Some Trump," "It's a Purity Ring Thang," "It's a Shotgun Wedding, Literally," "Not on Our Watch," "Shout at the Devil," "Trump: The Rock & Roll Muse"

Vocativ: "Muslim? No Guns for You"

IMAGE CREDITS

All cartoons by **TED RALL**.

Front cover photo by mikeledray/Shutterstock.com.

Trump band photo courtesy Brothers N Arms.

Harmon on the Mexican border photo by Brad Kuehnemuth.

Gun store wedding photos courtesy The Gun Store Las Vegas.

All other photos by **HARMON LEON**.

ABOUT THE AUTHORS

HARMON LEON is a journalist, comedian, and the author of eight books, including *The Harmon Chronicles* and *Republican Like Me*, which both won Independent Publisher Awards for humor. His latest title is *Tribespotting: Undercover Cult(ure) Stories*. Leon has appeared on *This American Life*, *The Howard Stern Show*, *Penn and Teller: Bullshit!*, *Last Call with Carson Daly*, MSNBC, and the BBC. He has performed critically-acclaimed solo comedy shows at venues around the world, including The Edinburgh Festival, Melbourne Comedy Festival, and Montreal's Just for Laughs. His writing can be found in *Vice*, *The Nation*, *Esquire*, *Ozy*, *National Geographic*, *The Guardian*, *Wired*, and more. Leon is the producer of a recent Official Selection at the Sundance Film Festival and the host of a popular podcast: *Comedy History 101*. Visit him online at www.harmonleon.com.

TED RALL has worked in almost every aspect of cartooning. His syndicated editorial cartoons for Andrews McMeel Syndication have appeared in publications like *The New York Times*, *Rolling Stone*, *Washington Post*, and *Village Voice* since the 1990s and have earned him two RFK Journalism Awards and a Pulitzer finalistship. He has done local- and state-issue cartoons for *The Asbury Park Press*, *Las Vegas Review-Journal*, *Harrisburg Patriot-News*, and *The Los Angeles Times* and humor cartoons for *MAD* magazine. Rall was a top editor at United Media and continues to edit cartoons for a variety of publications and cartoonists. He is also a widely-circulated syndicated opinion columnist for Creators Syndicate and has published twenty books, including collections of cartoons and essays, original graphic novels, war correspondence, adventure, travel, and political biographies. Rall's best-known books are the Gen X manifesto *Revenge of the Latchkey Kids*, the war travelogue *To Afghanistan and Back*, and the political bios *Snowden* and *Bernie*. His latest title is *Francis, the People's Pope*. Rall lives in New York. Find his work at www.rall.com.

www.ingramcontent.com/pod-product-compliance
Lightning Source LLC
Chambersburg PA
CBHW031147020426
42333CB00013B/550